# Contents

# About this Book

**Essential *London*** is divided into five sections to cover the most important aspects of your visit to London.

**Viewing London** pages 5–14
An introduction to London by the author
London's Features
Essence of London
The Shaping of London
Peace and Quiet
London's Famous

**Top Ten** pages 15–26
The author's choice of the Top Ten places to see in London, listed in alphabetical order, each with practical information.

**What to See** pages 27–90
Two sections: Central London and Outer London and Beyond, each with its own brief introduction and an alphabetical listing of the main attractions
Practical information
Snippets of 'Did you know…' information
6 suggested walks
2 features

**Where To…** pages 91–116
Detailed listings of the best places to eat, stay, shop, take the children and be entertained.

**Practical Matters** pages 117–24
A highly visual section containing essential travel information.

**Maps**
All map references are to the individual maps found in the What to See section of this guide.
For example, Buckingham Palace has the reference ➕ 28C2 – indicating the page on which the map is located and the grid square in which the royal residence is to be found. A list of the maps that have been used in this travel guide can be found in the index.

**Prices**
Where appropriate, an indication of the cost of an establishment is given by £ signs:
**£££** denotes higher prices, **££** denotes average prices, while **£** denotes lower charges.

**Star Ratings**
Most of the places described in this book have been given a separate rating:

| | |
|---|---|
| ✪✪✪ | Do not miss |
| ✪✪ | Highly recommended |
| ✪ | Worth seeing |

# Essential
# London

## by Paul Murphy

Paul Murphy's first London guide won the
London Tourist Board award for the best
London guidebook of the year. Since then he
has written over 25 guidebooks to holiday
destinations all over the world and has
contributed to many more books and
publications. London, however, is still one of
his favourite places.

Above: *a Chelsea pensioner*

**AA Publishing**

Above: *on guard in Whitehall*

Front cover: *sunset over Waterloo Bridge; a Beefeater; Eurostar*
Back cover: *food at Fortnum & Mason*

**Written by Paul Murphy**

Produced by AA Publishing.
© The Automobile Association 1999
Maps © The Automobile Association 1999
Reprinted May 1999

Distributed in the United Kingdom by AA Publishing, Norfolk House, Priestley Road, Basingstoke, Hampshire, RG24 9NY.

A CIP catalogue record for this book is available from the British Library.

ISBN 0 7495 1918 5

Published by AA Publishing, a trading name of Automobile Association Developments Limited, whose registered office is Norfolk House, Priestley Road, Basingstoke, Hampshire, RG24 9NY.
Registered number 1878835.

Colour separation: Pace Colour, Southampton
Printed and bound in Italy by Printer Trento srl

**The AA Hotel Booking Service**
This new service, provided exclusively for AA personal members, is a FREE, fast and easy way to find a place to stay for your short break, business trip or holiday. With your membership number to hand, call us now on 0990 050505 and let us know your requirements.

Find out more about AA Publishing and the wide range of services the AA provides by visiting our web site at www.theaa.co.uk

# Viewing
# London

Above: *Trafalgar Square*
Right: *City policeman*

# Paul Murphy's London

London may be the oldest of the modern world's great cities, with an exceptionally high proportion of ancient buildings, but it is also changing and evolving into a fresher, more vibrant destination for visitors. Nearly 40 years on from London's Swinging Sixties, the national and international press are telling us that once again this is the place to be.

Leading the world in fashion, music and the arts, London is now also rated as the restaurant capital of the world. Hyperbole or reality? Just look around. Ten years ago, when I wrote my first guide to London, the vast majority of visitor attractions were 'look but don't touch', you couldn't get a decent meal without paying the earth, a

**Seeing London**

If you want to see London, as opposed to just 'doing' its sights, then put on your walking shoes. The bus and the tube have their uses but you can cover a surprising amount of the central area quite comfortably on foot. It is rarely worth taking the tube for fewer than three stops. The best bits of buildings are often at first-floor level, so keep glancing upwards.

cappuccino was still an exotic novelty, beer or wine was off limits for much of the day, and the only way to get into Buckingham Palace was to scale its walls.

Today, London is more European, more worldly, more open in its outlook. The great London institutions of the British Museum, the Tower of London, the museums of South Kensington and the Royal Opera House have all recently undergone (or are currently in the process of) major improvements, and London's developing South Bank and Docklands are also springing to life. Meanwhile, visitors returning to the capital can rest assured that the unsung heroes of London life – the quiet leafy squares, the parks and its myriad tiny unspoilt churches, pubs and shops – soldier timelessly on.

Above: *Narrowboats on the Regent's Canal, built in 1820 to link London's docks to the city of Birmingham*

Right: *Steel and glass at Canary Wharf, the heart of London's new 'City on the Water'*

6

# London's Features

## Geography
• London is the largest city in Europe, a ragged oval stretching over 50km (30 miles) across. However, most of 'Visitors' London' is condensed into Inner London, the area bounded by the Underground's Circle Line (➤ 72).
• The best way to see the capital is by a combination of underground (tube) and walking.

## Locals and Visitors
• London's population reached a peak of around 8.6 million in 1939 then declined slowly to below 7 million in 1983. Only recently has it started to grow again.
• Formerly the world's most populous conurbation, London now ranks number ten in the world. By contrast, visitor numbers have been booming.
• In 1991 London registered 16 million visitors (ie those staying at least one night); by 1995 this figure had increased to 24 million.
• London is a cosmopolitan city, with 20 per cent of its population comprising non-white ethnic groups.

### Problems
• Westminster Council (who deal with the most-visited part of the capital) remove 90 tons of rubbish per day from its streets.
• London holds the richest and poorest segments of the British population – seven out of ten of the country's most deprived local authorities are in the capital.

### Traffic Congestion
The average vehicle speed in London is 16kph – not much faster than it was in 1900! No wonder then that some 5 million people per day choose to ride on the bus and tube network.

## Government
• Londoners have only recently voted to restore city-wide government. Political wrangling in the 1980s had led to the previous Greater London Council being abolished by central government.
• Most local decisions are devolved to 32 borough councils.
• Croydon is the largest borough with over 315,000 residents. The City of London, covering the square mile in the financial centre, is the smallest with barely 4,000.

Above: *The Houses of Parliament, once described by Tsar Nicholas I as 'a dream in stone'*

# Essence of London

London is such a varied and cosmopolitan city that there is a bewildering choice of things to do and see. Perhaps inevitably, visitors feel compelled to tick off its major sights at breakneck speed, but this is no way to get the flavour of the city. The key is not to rush, not to feel you have to see it all (you never will) and not to overlook the simple indigenous pleasures of London. Just for a day or two, forget the museums, the historical attractions, and especially the crowded West End stores. Instead, rummage through a street market stall, stroll in the parks, enjoy a pint in a theme-free pub – in short, be a local.

Below: *Sandwiches in the park and market stall browsing are the locals' ways of spending their lunch hour*

# THE 10 ESSENTIALS

*If you have only a short time to visit London, or would like to get a real flavour of the city, here are the essentials:*

- **Ride on the top deck of a London bus** – still a great way to see the capital. The Big Bus Company operate excellent tours, or take the regular service (No 11) from Chelsea to Bank.
- **Cruise on the Thames** – London's most under-utilised highway is the perfect route to Greenwich, and the journey is accompanied by a lively commentary.
- **Relax in the park** when the traffic noise grates and your feet ache; escape to Hyde Park, Kensington Gardens, St James's Park or Regent's Park.
- **Join a walking tour** and let a professional guide take you by the hand and lead you through the streets of London. It is the best and most enjoyable way to learn about the capital – and cheap too. Pick up a flyer from a tourist information office or see *Time Out* for details.

- **Take afternoon tea** – the quintessential British afternoon pastime (▶ 93).
- **Attend a church concert** – even the least God-fearing of folk will find this an uplifting experience (▶ 113).
- **Enjoy the view from Waterloo Bridge** to see St Paul's and the London skyline at their very best.
- **Visit a traditional London pub**, although it's hard to tell the phoneys from the real thing these days (▶ 53, 97 for some suggestions).
- **Visit a street market** – two of the best are Brick Lane and Portobello Road, held on Sundays (▶ 108–9 for more suggestions). All London life is there!
- **Visit the Inns of Court** – not a 'sight' as such, but an astonishing oasis in the heart of the city and a glimpse of 'olde London' that few locals (let alone visitors) ever see (▶ 47–8).

*Transports of delight – the only thing better than the top deck of a London bus is the top deck of a London boat*

# The Shaping of London

**AD 43**
The Roman emperor Claudius invades Britain and establishes the deep-water port of Londinium.

*c***60–200**
The Romans build an imperial city and in around AD 200 erect a wall around Londinium. The population reaches 45–50,000.

**410**
Romans finally withdraw, leaving Britons to defend themselves. Germanic tribes begin to colonise most of England.

**851–980**
Vikings invade, occupy and destroy much of London. In 886 King Alfred recaptures and rebuilds the city, establishing it as an international trading centre, but in 980 the Vikings retake it.

**1066**
The Norman Conquest. William I defeats King Harold at the Battle of Hastings and is crowned King of England at Westminster Abbey.

**1176–1209**
London Bridge is the first stone bridge to be built in the capital. In 1192 the first Mayor of London, Henry Fitz Ailwyn, is elected.

**1265**
The first meeting of 'the Commons' marks the beginnings of the Parliamentary system.

**1348**
The Black Death, a cocktail of various plagues spread by infected fleas on rats, kills some 75 million people across Eurasia and wipes out around 25–30,000 Londoners (roughly half the population).

**1485–1603**
Under Tudor rule London becomes Europe's fastest-growing city, with dramatic development of trade and commerce. Around 1590 London's original 'Theatreland' is developed on the South Bank in Southwark, and the West End also takes shape.

**1642–49**
The English Civil War ends with the execution of Charles I at Whitehall in 1649. Cromwell's forces assume power until the restoration of the monarchy in 1660.

**1665**
The Great Plague, London's second catastrophic bubonic plague, ravages London and claims the lives of over 100,000 people.

*St Paul's is destroyed in the Great Fire of London*

10

*The Great Exhibition in the Crystal Palace*

**1666**
The Great Fire of London burns down 80 per cent of the city's buildings.

**1750**
Westminster Bridge becomes the second bridge across the Thames in London.

**1801**
The first London census records a population of over 1 million, making it the world's most populous conurbation.

**1811–17**
As the population continues to explode 14 more bridges are built across the Thames.

**1829**
Sir Robert Peel establishes the capital's first police force – the Metropolitan Police. The first London bus service commences.

**1834**
The Palace of Westminster (Houses of Parliament) burns down.

**1849–58**
Insanitary living conditions lead to a cholera epidemic which kills 14,000, and river pollution causes 'The Great Stink', which prompts the building of London's first sewerage system. The Great Exhibition opens, in 1851, in Hyde Park.

**1863**
The world's first urban underground railway runs from Farringdon Street to Edgware Road.

**1939–45**
During the Blitz of 1940–41 London is bombed for 57 consecutive nights causing 9,500 deaths and much destruction.

**1960s**
The Beatles are at the forefront of 'Swinging London' and world fashion focuses on Carnaby Street and the King's Road.

**1981**
Work begins to revive London's Docklands.

**1994**
Eurostar trains connect London and Paris via the Channel Tunnel.

**1996**
An IRA bomb devastates a large part of central Docklands.

**1998**
Final plate is layed on the roof of the Milennium Dome in Greenwich.

# Peace & Quiet

Like all big cities, London can become extremely wearing after just a short time so it's good to know that it has proportionately more green spaces than any other metropolis, plus a fair number of unusual bolt holes.

*Hampstead Heath is Londoners' favourite spot for countryside walks without leaving town*

## Parks and Gardens

**Battersea Park** What could be more restful than a stroll in a park with a Peace Pagoda of its very own? There's also a children's zoo and a boating pond. Completely off the tourist path yet visible from Chelsea Embankment, the park (and pagoda) is just a few minutes' walk across Albert Bridge (➤ 36).

**Chelsea Physic Garden** This charming small botanical garden was founded by the Society of Apothecaries; its name means 'of things natural' (➤ 36).

**Greenwich Park** Lovely gardens, a boating lake and a wonderful view from the top of the hill (➤ 81).

**Hampstead Heath/Richmond Park** You'll always be able to find space of your own on London's largest heath (➤ 43) or in its largest and wildest park (➤ 87).

**Wimbledon Common** over 400 hectares of open space in south London, with parkland, woodland and heath.

**Hampton Court** The beautiful grounds and gardens start to fill up at weekends and holidays, but otherwise are delightfully tranquil (➤ 85).

**Hyde Park** Too central and too well-known to offer real peace and quiet, but wander into the centre of the park on a weekday in school term time and you might just find a measure of tranquillity. You can hire rowing boats on the Serpentine (➤ 45).

**Kew Gardens** The perfect place for those with green fingers – though it does get busy on Sundays (➤ 86).

**The Regent's Canal** Take a traditional narrowboat to explore London's backwaters. The most popular excursion is from Little Venice to Camden Lock, with London Zoo en route. London Waterbus Company ☎ 0171-482 2550 or Jason's Trip ☎ 0171-286 6101.

*The statue of Peter Pan in Kensington Gardens was erected overnight as a surprise for the local children*

## Urban Escapes
Even in the heart of London you'll find unexpected places of calm. Many churches, particularly in the City, have restful small gardens. At lunchtimes free concerts are often given. St Paul's Churchyard, in Covent Garden (➤ 18), is a notable oasis and Postman's Park, in Aldersgate (near the Museum of London) is a particularly touching spot with a wall of plaques dedicated to members of the public who died in heroic acts of self-sacrifice.

Under-visited galleries and museums include Apsley House (➤ 32), Dickens House (➤ 39), Leighton House (➤ 50), the National Army Museum (➤ 59) and the Wallace Collection (➤ 76).

## Thames Path
Officially launched in 1996 the Thames Path is a footpath which allows walkers to follow the Thames all the way from its source (in Gloucestershire) to the Thames Barrier. Follow the South Bank while in central London, though both sides of the river are accessible. National Trail Officer ☎ (01865) 810224.

*Little bits of greenery are found in unexpected places, here next to St Paul's Cathedral*

13

# London's Famous

## Charles Dickens

Born on the south coast in Portsmouth in 1812, Charles Dickens came to London in 1823. His early career as a lawyer and a reporter, combined with the financial hardships suffered by his father (who spent a short time in a debtors' prison), shaped his conceptions of the harsh realities and social injustices of London. His first real writing success, under the pen-name Boz, was *The Pickwick Papers*, published in serial form during 1836–7. He went on to write a further 13 major novels, including *A Christmas Carol*, *Oliver Twist*, *Nicholas Nickleby* and *David Copperfield* and died in 1870 leaving the last one incomplete. A superb orator who took his stories on tour, much as a musician gives concerts, Dickens was the finest writer of his time and arguably the greatest-ever English novelist. The vitality and colour with which he invested his characters and his ability to tell a story which captured the spirit of the age made him indeed 'The Inimitable' – his own immodest sobriquet! (➤ 39).

## Sir Christopher Wren

*Right: Sir Christopher Wren is buried in St Paul's Cathedral, his most famous work*
*Below: Her Majesty Queen Elizabeth II*

A brilliant polymath, Christopher Wren (1632–1723) began his career as an astronomer and mathematician before turning to architecture. In 1669 he was appointed Surveyor of Rebuilding after the Great Fire of London. However, contrary to popular legend, his grand plans for a cohesive new London foundered on the complex network and politics of land ownership. Instead he turned his immense talents and energy to St Paul's Cathedral (➤ 22) and to City churches.

## Queen Elizabeth II

London's most famous resident – from April to mid-August at least – is Elizabeth Mountbatten-Windsor, better known as Her Majesty Queen Elizabeth II (born 1926). During the rest of the year she spends time at Windsor Castle and her other palaces. Despite her recent family problems – fire at Windsor Castle, the breakdown of her children's marriages, the death of Diana and a widespread appraisal of the modern role of the royals – the Queen herself remains inviolable.

# Top Ten

Above: *bustling Covent Garden*
Right: *Victoria Memorial*

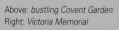

# 1
# British Museum

✝ 29D4

✉ Great Russell Street, Bloomsbury

☎ 0171-636 1555
Recorded information
0171-580 1788

🕐 Mon–Sat 10–5, Sun 2:30–6. Closed 24–26 Dec, 1 Jan, Good Fri, May Day bank hol

🍴 Café (£), Restaurant (££)

Ⓜ Holborn, Tottenham Court Road, Russell Square

🚌 Regent Street 3, 6, 12, 13, 15, 53, 59, 88, 159; Piccadilly 9, 14, 19, 22b, 23, 38; New Bond Street southbound and Berkeley Street northbound 8

♿ Excellent. Access enquiries ☎ 0171-323 8299; Artsline, voice and minicom ☎ 0171-388 2227. Leaflet detailing facilities available at reception

✋ Free

❓ Highlights tour Mon–Sat 11:15, 2:15; Sun 3, 3:30. Eye Openers tours (free) hourly every day; pick up a leaflet for details

*The British Museum holds what is probably the greatest collection of antiquities in the world, and is also the country's most visited cultural attraction.*

Founded in 1753 from the collection of Sir Hans Sloane, the BM (as it is known to its regulars) has occupied its present site since 1823. Current upheavals, however, which include the recent relocation of the British Library and the construction of a spectacular Great Court entrance, are as drastic as anything the museum has seen. As a consequence visitors can expect disruption, even though most exhibits will remain unaffected. The following are just a few of the BM's greatest and most popular treasures. Pick up a floor plan to locate them.

Starting on the ground floor, the sculptures from the Parthenon (the Elgin Marbles) are widely held to be the greatest works of their kind from ancient Greece. The adjacent Nereid Monument, from Xanthos, Turkey, is a striking reconstructed temple. For more breathtaking sculptures on a monumental scale see the Assyrian human-headed winged bulls of Khorsabad. The museum

The Progress of Civilisation *is carved above the portico of the 'greatest jackdaw's meet in the world'*

boasts the greatest collection of Egyptology outside Cairo and the majestic exhibits in the huge Egyptian Hall will linger long in the memory. They include the famous Rosetta Stone, which enabled scholars to decipher the meaning of hieroglyphics. Not so renowned but equally worth while are the Oriental Collection (particularly the Indian sculptures) and the Mexican Gallery, both of which contain outstandingly beautiful works of art. In the British Library Galleries the Magna Carta is the most popular draw, but another 'must see' are the remarkable Lindisfarne Gospels.

On the upper floors follow the crowds to the macabre Egyptian mummies and the preserved un-mummified body of 'Ginger'. In the Prehistoric and Romano-British sections, highlights include Lindow Man, the Sutton Hoo Treasure, the Mildenhall Treasure and the Lewis Chessmen. Close by, the Clocks and Watches collection, from the 16th to the 20th century, is one of the finest in the world. Be there on the hour when the clocks chime in unison. Easily overlooked among a welter of antiquities from Greece and Rome is the Portland Vase, a priceless example of the art of glass making.

Below: *This 4th-century Roman silver bowl is part of the museum's famous Mildenhall Treasure*

# 2
# Covent Garden Piazza

✚ 29D3

🚇 Covent Garden

🍴 A wide choice (£–££) of cafés and restaurants

*London's most continental square, is thronged with shoppers and sightseers by day, and with theatregoers and revellers by night.*

Covent Garden Piazza was laid out in the Italian style in 1630 by Inigo Jones. Initially it was a very fashionable address, but from 1670 onwards, with the advent of the main London fruit, flower and vegetable market, it was driven down-market and developed into a notorious red-light area. In 1830 its handsome centrepiece iron and glass hall was erected and the market continued trading at Covent Garden until 1974, when, finally defeated by transport logistics, it moved south of the river to Vauxhall. The site was then developed as a pedestrianised area, accommodating dozens of small shops and restaurants.

Today, only some arcading and St Paul's Church remain of the original Piazza. By the church portico top-class buskers (licensed by the Covent Garden authorities) entertain large crowds daily. It was here, in 1662, that England's first ever Punch and Judy show was staged. St Paul's is known as the Actor's Church because of the large number of memorials (and graves) of screen and stage stars it holds. It is well worth a look inside and its garden is a remarkably peaceful oasis amid the general hubbub.

The major museums around the Piazza are the London Transport Museum (► 54) and the Theatre Museum (► 71), but there is also the splendidly eccentric, very witty Cabaret Mechanical Theatre exhibition of automatons, in the pit of the market building. For details of the Royal Opera House and the area's theatres (► 112–15).

*Covent Garden's Central Market is now packed with fashionable shops and eateries*

# 3

# Houses of Parliament (Palace of Westminster)

*The home of the Mother of Parliaments and a masterpiece of Victorian Gothic, with over 1,000 rooms and the world's most famous clock tower.*

The Houses of Parliament, seat of British government, dates back to c1050, when William the Conqueror built his Palace of Westminster on this site. It evolved into a parliament around the mid-13th century and continued to be used as a royal palace until 1512, when Henry VIII moved his court to Whitehall. In 1834 a disastrous fire burned everything above ground (with the exception of Westminster Hall, the cloisters and the Jewel Tower), and so construction began of the building that you see today. The principal architect was Charles Barry, though the flamboyant ubiquitous Gothic decorative touches are the work of his assistant, Augustus Pugin. By 1860, some 20 years later than planned and around £1.4 million over budget, it was virtually complete. The best-known part of the Houses is the clock tower, referred to as Big Ben – though to be precise this is the name of the great 13-ton bell which chimes every hour. After dark a light above the clock face indicates when Parliament is 'sitting' (when it is in session).

✚ 29D3

✉ Public entrance on St Margaret Street

☎ Public Information Office 0171-219 4272 (Commons), 0171-219 3107 (Lords)

Members of the public may attend debates at both Houses.

Westminster

3, 11, 12, 24, 77a, 211

Waterloo

♿ for access ☎ 0171-219 3700

✋ Free

The modern Houses of Parliament divide principally into two debating chambers. The House of Commons comprises Members of Parliament (MPs) who are the elected representatives of the British people. Their functions are legislation and (as opposition) government scrutiny. The non-elected House of Lords is an apolitical body of the great and good, who examine proposed legislation from the Commons and also act as the highest Appeal Court in the land.

*Richard I ('the Lionheart'), the heroic English crusader king, in Old Palace Yard outside Parliament*

# 4
# National Gallery

29D3

Trafalgar Square

0171-747 2885

Mon–Sat 10–6 (Wed until 8), Sun 12–6. Closed 24–26 Dec, 1 Jan, Good Fri

Café (£), Brasserie (££)

Charing Cross

3, 6, 9, 11, 12, 13, 15, 23, 24, 29, 53, 53, 77a, 88, 91, 94, 109, 139, 159, 176

Charing Cross, Leicester Square, Embankment

Regent Street

Excellent

Free

*Home to one of the finest and most comprehensive collections of Western art in the world, the National Gallery houses over 2,000 paintings.*

The collection is divided chronologically, with the Sainsbury Wing housing the oldest paintings, from 1260 to 1510. Two of the most famous works are *The Virgin and Child* cartoon by Leonardo da Vinci and *Venus and Mars* by Botticelli. *The Doge* by Giovanni Bellini is considered the greatest-ever Venetian portrait. Less famous but equally worth while are *The Wilton Diptych* (by an unknown artist), *The Battle of San Romano* by Ucello, *The Baptism of Christ* by Piero della Francesca and *The Arnolfini Portrait* by Jan Van Eyck.

The West Wing progresses to 1600 and includes *The Entombment* (unfinished), which is the gallery's sole work by Michelangelo. Two famous mythology paintings are *Bacchus and Ariadne* by Titian and *Allegory with Venus and Cupid* by Bronzino. More prosaic masterpieces include Holbein's *Ambassadors* and *Pope Julius II* by Raphael.

The North Wing deals with the 17th century. Among its 15 or so Rembrandts is the sorrowful *Self Portrait at the Age of 63* (that same year he died a pauper). Contrast this with the pompous *Equestrian Portrait of Charles I* by Van Dyck, and the charming *Le Chapeau de Paille* (Straw Hat) portrait by Rubens. *Young Woman Standing at a Virginal* by Vermeer, *The Rokeby Venus* by Velázquez and *Enchanted Castle* by Claude are also worth seeking out.

The East Wing (1700–1920) contains a whole host of popular favourites: *Sunflowers* by Van Gogh; *Bathers at Asnières* by Seurat; *Parapluies* (Umbrellas) by Renoir; and from the British school, *Hay-Wain* by Constable and *Fighting Temeraire* by J M W Turner.

*The National Gallery houses the country's most popular art collection, attracting over 3 million visitors per year*

# 5
# Natural History Museum

*A family favourite where dinosaurs roar back to life, an earthquake shakes the ground and creepy-crawlies make the flesh tingle.*

Moving with the times: animatronic meat-eaters in Kensington

To thousands of children the Natural History Museum is 'the Dinosaur Museum', and no visit would be complete without poring over the superbly displayed skeletons of the museum's world-famous collection. There's much more here than just prehistoric monsters, however. Highest of all on the heavyweights list is the blue whale. It may only be a model, but what a model, measuring over 28m with a real 25m skeleton alongside. Around here there is a vast array of stuffed specimens to ponder on while at the other end of the size spectrum, children (if not adults) will love the 'Creepy-Crawlies' exhibition. For more ethereal concepts, visit the state-of-the-art Ecology display and gingerly examine the workings of your own body in the Human Biology section. One of the museum's greatest attractions is its very structure, built in neo-Gothic cathedral style by Alfred Waterhouse in 1880. The Cromwell Road frontage is magnificent and there is a wealth of interior detail to enjoy.

Once you've seen life on earth, explore the adjacent Earth Galleries (formerly known as the Geological Museum) which tell the story of the earth's formation and its on-going upheavals. This is a far cry from the old museum's displays of rocks in dusty glass cases, though its wonderful collection of gemstones remains a highlight. The main attraction is the Power Within exhibitions where the ground-shaking sensations of a real earthquake are simulated and audio visuals show breathtaking footage of volcanoes and their devastating effects on everyday objects.

✝ 28A1

✉ Cromwell Road (Life Galleries), Exhibition Road (Earth Galleries)

☎ 0171-938 9123

🕐 Mon–Sat 10–5:50, Sun 11–5:50. Closed 23–26 Dec

🍴 Gallery Restaurant (££), Waterhouse Café (£)

🚇 South Kensington

🚌 74

♿ Excellent

✋ Expensive. Free after 4:30 Mon–Fri, after 5 Sat, Sun

❓ Free tours: museum highlights hourly 11–4; Wildlife Garden May–Sep (45 min), twice a day. Book for both at Life Galleries information desk. Also behind-the-scenes tours (phone to arrange)

# 6
# St Paul's Cathedral

✝ 29E3

✉ St Paul's Churchyard

☎ 0171-246 4128

🕓 Open to visitors
Mon–Sat 8:30–4

🍴 Café in crypt (£)

Ⓟ St Paul's

🚌 11, 15, 17, 23, 26

🚆 Cannon Street

♿ Floor and crypt
excellent. Galleries
inaccessible

✋ Cathedral and crypt
moderate. Galleries
moderate

❓ Self-guided audio tours,
90-min guided tours

*The Mother Church of the Diocese of London and the supreme work of Sir Christopher Wren, one of the world's great architects.*

Work began on the present St Paul's Cathedral after the Great Fire of 1666 had destroyed its predecessor, Old St Paul's. Its foundation stone was laid by Christopher Wren in 1675 and after 35 years of sweat and toil (during which time Wren's salary was halved as punishment for slow progress) it was completed in 1710. Take time to enjoy the magnificent west front before entering the church. Inside it is surprisingly light and airy, largely as a result of the use of plain glass windows (much favoured by Wren) which were installed to replace the old stained glass destroyed during World War II.

Go past the huge monument to the Duke of Wellington and stop in the middle of the transepts to look skywards to the wonderful dome – one of the three largest in the world. Move on to the choir, the most lavishly decorated part of the church, and don't miss the scorch-marked statue of John Donne (poet and Dean of Old St Paul's). This is one of London's very few monuments to survive the Great Fire of 1666.

Descend to the crypt, where you will find the tombs of some of Britain's greatest heroes, including the Duke of Wellington and Lord Nelson, and, of course, Christopher Wren himself. Return to the church and begin the ascent to the galleries. The justifiably famous Whispering Gallery, whose remarkable acoustics will carry a whisper quite audibly from one side to the other, is perched 30m above the floor. Finally, after a total of 530 steps, you will reach the Golden Gallery, where you will be rewarded with one of the finest views in all London. Return to the cathedral floor and contemplate William Holman Hunt's uplifting masterpiece, *The Light of the World*.

*Don't miss St Paul's by night, when it is dramatically floodlit*

# 7
# Science Museum

*Don't be put off by the name or the concept of a museum of science. This is an exhibition of how things work and how technology has evolved.*

The Science Museum is one of the world's finest collections of its kind. It is a huge undertaking, however, and you can't hope to see and understand everything here in a single visit. On the other hand there are so many pieces which are landmarks of industrial history, technological milestones, works of art, or just amazing objects in their own right, there really is something that everyone can identify with and admire.

To see the best of the collection in one visit buy the excellent museum guidebook which will navigate you through the 'must-see' exhibits such as Stephenson's *Rocket*, Edison's early lamps, the ill-fated Ford Edsel motorcar, the prototype computer (the dauntingly huge Babbage's Difference Engine), the Apollo 10 Command module, the first iron lung, ancient orreries, and many other famous technological landmarks.

The Science Museum is famous for its pioneering interactive hands-on areas and adults with children should start down in the basement, then progress to Launch Pad. Here youngsters can discover how machines and gadgets work. Other family favourites include the Flight Galleries, featuring a whole array of historic aircraft, many of them slung dramatically from the ceiling. For sheer spectacle it's hard to beat the East Hall, where some of the great beam-and-steam behemoths which powered the Industrial Revolution still push and thrust their mighty workings.

If you have any energy left, the Wellcome History of Medicine on the top floor is a fascinating collection with an emphasis on ancient and tribal medicines, and features some blood-curdling practices.

*Stephenson's Rocket is a Science Museum favourite*

✚ 28A2

✉ Exhibition Road

☎ 0171-938 8008/8080/8000; minicom line 0171-938 9770; disabled persons enquiry line 0171-938 9788

🕐 Daily 10–6. Closed 24–26 Dec

🍴 Museum café (£), picnic areas

Ⓟ South Kensington

🚌 9, 9A, 10, 14, 49, 52, 74, C1

♿ Excellent

✋ Moderate, free after 4:30

# 8
# Tower of London

✚ 29F3

✉ Tower of London

☎ 0171-709 0765

🕐 Mar–Oct Mon–Sat 9–5, Sun 10–5; Nov–Feb Tue–Sat 9–4, Sun–Mon 10–4.

🍴 Café (£)

Ⓜ Tower Hill

🚌 15, x15, 25, 42, 78, 100, D1, D9, D11

🚆 Fenchurch Street

♿ Tower staff very willing to help but inherent problems with old buildings. Phone in advance for details

💷 Very expensive

❓ Buy tickets in advance from any underground station to avoid waiting at the Tower entrance.

*London's foremost historical site, the Tower has served as castle, palace, prison, arsenal, jewel house and site of execution over its 900-year lifespan.*

The oldest part of the Tower of London is the great central keep. Known as the White Tower, it was begun by William I in 1078 to intimidate his newly conquered subjects; the rest of the fortifications took on their present shape in the late 13th and early 14th centuries.

All tours begin with a short, highly entertaining guided walk led by one of the Tower's traditionally dressed Yeoman Warders (Beefeaters). They gleefully relate stories of imprisonment, torture and intrigue, while taking you past a few of the 20 towers, the famous ravens ('only so long as they stay will the White Tower stand'), Traitors' Gate and the execution site of Tower Green. Here, among others, Henry VIII's wives Anne Boleyn and Catherine Howard lost their heads. After visiting the adjacent Chapel of St Peter ad Vincula you are left to explore by yourself and join the inevitable queues at the Jewel House and the White Tower. Both are well worth the wait. The former houses the Crown Jewels, many of which date back to the 17th-century Restoration period and are still used by the present Queen and royal family. The White Tower is home to part of the magnificent Royal Armouries and also includes the beautiful, very atmospheric 11th-century Chapel of St John. Also highly recommended is a visit to the restored rooms of the medieval palace.

# 9
# Victoria & Albert Museum

*The V&A is not only Britain's national museum of art and design, but comprises the greatest collection of decorative arts in the world.*

The V&A was founded in 1852 with the objective of exhibiting the world's very best examples of design and applied arts in order to inspire students and crafts people. It has subsequently grown to include an astonishing and immense diversity of objects. Your first task is to arm yourself with a map and index to help you navigate the 13km labyrinth of stairs and corridors.

Perhaps the V&A's greatest treasures are the Raphael Cartoons, seven huge tapestry designs that have become even more famous than the actual tapestries themselves (which hang in the Sistine Chapel in Rome). While on the ground floor, don't miss the Italian Renaissance sculptures; the Cast Courts, full-size plaster casts of fascinating European masterpieces including Trajan's Column and Michelangelo's *David*; the Morris, Poynter and Gamble Rooms, the V&A's original refreshment rooms and masterpieces of Victorian decoration; a dip into the multifarious treasures of the Orient – from China, Japan, Islam and India; and the Dress Collection.

On level B is the Jewellery Gallery, beautifully displayed under Fort Knox-like security conditions. Close by and also worth seeing for its setting alone is the Silver Gallery, while on level C the sparkling new Glass Gallery is a wonderful exhibition of glass spanning a period of 4,000 years. Tucked away in the Henry Cole Wing are some of John Constable's best works.

28A2

Entrances on Brompton Road, Cromwell Road

0171-938 8500; 0171-938 8441 24-hour information line

Mon 12–5:45, Tue–Sun 10–5:45. From Easter through summer reopens on Wed eve 6:30–9:30. Closed 24–26 Dec

Excellent cafés (£) and restaurant (££) on premises. Sun jazz brunch (11–3) in the New Restaurant

South Kensington

C1, 14, 74 stop outside Cromwell Road entrance

Excellent. Pick up a detailed leaflet from information desk

Moderate; free daily 4:30–5:45

Tours: introductory tours Mon 12:15, 2, 3; Tue–Sun 11, 12, 2, 3; special interest tours Mon 1:30, 2:30; Tue–Sun 11:30, 1:30, 2:30. Note: all the British Design Galleries and the Ceramics Galleries are closed for refurbishment until 2001

Left: *The V&A was opened by Queen Victoria in 1857; the central tower is modelled on an imperial crown*
Opposite: *the Tower of London protects the Crown Jewels*

# 10
# Westminster Abbey

✝ 29D2

✉ Dean's Yard

☎ Abbey 0171-222 7110; chapter house, museum, Pyx Chamber 0171-222 5897

🕐 Nave, cloisters daily 8–6; abbey Mon–Fri 9–4:45, Sat 9–2:45. Last admission 1 hour before closing time. No sightseeing on Sun; Pyx Chamber and museum daily 10:30–4

🍴 Coffee stands outside abbey and in cloisters

Ⓜ Westminster, St James's Park

🚌 3, 11, 24, 77a, 88, 211

♿ Ramped wheelchair access available

✋ Cloisters free; abbey moderate; chapter house, museum, Pyx Chamber combined ticket cheap/moderate

❓ Guided tours: Apr–Oct Mon–Fri 10, 11, 2, 2:30, 3 (except Fri), Sat 10, 11, 12:30; Nov–Mar 10, 11, 2, 3 (except Fri), Sat 10, 11, 12:30. Tours restricted to 25 persons. Bookings may be made in advance. ☎ 0171–222 7110. Tour 🎫 cheap/moderate, additional, includes admission to chapter house, museum and Pyx Chamber. Audio tour available (🎧 cheap, additional)

*The coronation site of British royalty, the last resting place of kings, queens and celebrities this architectural triumph is awash with history.*

Westminster Abbey was founded c1050 by Edward the Confessor who was the first king to be buried here. William the Conqueror was crowned king in the abbey on Christmas Day in 1066 and so began a tradition that was last re-enacted in 1953 when the coronation of the present monarch, Queen Elizabeth II, took place here.

The present building dates mostly from the 13th century and the reign of Henry III. The nave is chock-a-block with graves and monuments, none more famous than the Tomb of the Unknown Warrior who represents the 765,000 British servicemen killed in World War I, though the real glory of the abbey lies beyond the sumptuously carved and gilded screen (by which Isaac Newton and Charles Darwin lie) in the Royal Chapels. Here you will find the coronation chair and the often-magnificent tombs of dozens of royals. The abbey's *tour de force* lies at its easternmost point; Henry VII's Chapel, built between 1503 and 1519, with its sublime fan-vaulting. In the south transept is the famous Poets' Corner where many celebrated writers, musicians and artists are honoured.

Try and see the beautiful abbey precinct which includes the cloisters, the chapter house, the fascinating Westminster Abbey Museum (with contemporary royal wax effigies) and the Pyx ('money chest') Chamber.

*An ornate pulpit among Westminster Abbey's soaring arches*

# What to See

Above: *detail in Pall Mall*
Right: *letter box*

27

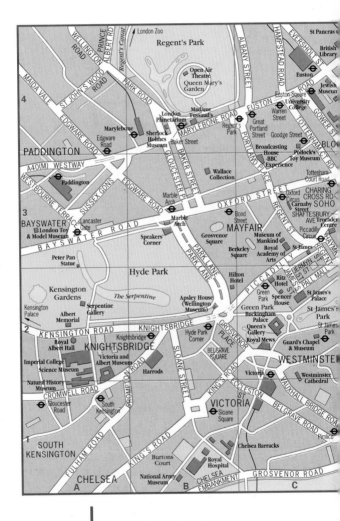

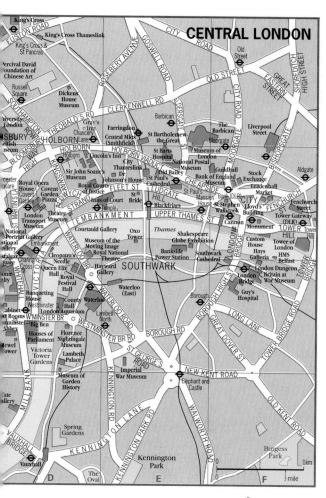

**CENTRAL LONDON**

King's Cross
EUSTON ROAD
King's Cross Thameslink
King's Cross & St Pancras
CITY ROAD
Old Street
GREAT EASTERN STREET
SHOREDITCH HIGH STREET
Percival David Foundation of Chinese Art
Russell Square
Dickens House Museum
ROSEBERY AVENUE
GOSWELL ROAD
OLD STREET
CITY ROAD
SOUTHAMPTON ROW
niversity London
ritish useum
CLERKENWELL RD
Barbican
ALDERSGATE
The Barbican
Liverpool Street
THEOBALD'S RD
Guy's Inn Chancery Lane
Farringdon
St Bartholemew the Great
Museum of London
BISHOPSGATE
HOLBORN
Central Mkt (Smithfield)
Moorgate
HIGH HOLBORN
St Barts Hospital
National Postal Museum
Aldgate
BLOOMSBURY
KINGSWAY
Holborn
Lincoln's Inn
City Thameslink
Old Bailey
Bank of England Museum
Stock Exchange
LUDGATE HILL
cester uare
Sir John Soane's Museum
Dr Johnson's House
St Paul's Cathedral
Leadenhall Market
Royal Opera House
Covent Garden
Royal Courts of Justice
St Paul's
CHEAPSIDE
Guildhall
FENCHURCH ST
Covent Garden Piazza
ST MARTIN'S LN
Inns of Court
FLEET ST
St Bride
Mansion House
Bank (DLR)
St Stephen Walbrook
Lloyd's Building
Fenchurch Street
STRAND
Temple
Blackfriars
CITY
CANNON
Monument
Tower Gateway (DLR)
London Transport Museum
ALDWYCH
Theatre
EMBANKMENT
UPPER THAMES ST
LONDON BRIDGE
Tower Hill
National Portrait Gallery
ational allery
Courtauld Gallery
Oxo Tower
Thames
Shakespeare Globe Exhibition
Custom House
Tower of London
TOWER HILL
Tower Hill
rafalgar quare
Embankment
Cleopatra's Needle
Museum of the Moving Image
Royal National Theatre
Bankside Power Station
Southwark Cathedral
Hays Galleria
HMS Belfast
TOWER BRIDGE
amiralty
Charing Cross
Queen Eliz Hall
Hayward Gallery
SOUTHWARK
London Bridge
London Dungeon
Britain at War Museum
WHITEHALL
Banqueting House
Royal Festival Hall
Waterloo (East)
Guy's Hospital
Westminster
County Hall
Waterloo
Borough
VICTORIA
Cabinet
r Rooms
stminster Abbey
Big Ben
London Aquarium
WATERLOO ROAD
Borough
BOROUGH HIGH STREET
W'MINSTER BR
Houses of Parliament
Florence Nightingale Museum
Waterloo North
LONG LANE
TOWER BRIDGE ROAD
ewel ower
WESTMINSTER BR RD
BOROUGH RD
GREAT DOVER ST
Victoria Tower Gardens
Lambeth Palace
MILLBANK
Museum of Garden History
LAMBETH ROAD
ST GEORGE'S ROAD
Imperial War Museum
NEW KENT ROAD
ate allery
KENNINGTON ROAD
KENNINGTON LANE
Elephant and Castle
OLD KENT ROAD
VAUXHALL BRIDGE
Spring Gardens
WALWORTH ROAD
Burgess Park
Vauxhall
KENNINGTON PARK ROAD
KENNINGTON PARK RD
Kennington Park
1km
The Oval
Kennington Park
½ mile
0

D        E        F

# London

London is one of the world's few truly great cities. Its depth of history is unrivalled by any other major capital, its shopping is the envy of Europe, and it is currently undergoing a renaissance in cuisine and fashion. With over 24 million visitors per year and one of the world's most cosmopolitan indigenous make-ups, it is a global melting pot, catering for all tastes and nationalities.

Of course, not all is perfect. Hotel prices are too high, the weather is unpredictable (so be prepared!) and the traffic is horrendous. On the other hand, London is a very civilised city. Life may be fast and sometimes impersonal, but it is very rarely aggressive and oases of calm – the parks, historic churches, museums, and hotels and department stores serving afternoon tea – are never more than a few steps away.

> *'Why, Sir, you find no man at all intellectual who is willing to leave London. No, Sir, when a man is tired of London, he is tired of life; for there is in London all that life can afford.'*

DR SAMUEL JOHNSON, (1777)

# Central London

**One of the questions asked by many first-time visitors to London is 'Where is the centre?' The simple answer is that as London has evolved from a series of villages it has many centres. However, the West End – a rather vague geographical term generally covering Piccadilly, Soho and Covent Garden – is the accepted hub of the city for shopping, eating, drinking and nightlife, as well as a good slice of sightseeing.**

*Trafalgar Square is the exact centre of London, from which all distances are measured*

For orientation purposes Trafalgar Square, with its landmark Nelson's Column, is a good place to start. To the north is the West End, and beyond that Bloomsbury, a leafy district of handsome squares and home of the British Museum. Due west from Trafalgar Square is Westminster and Whitehall, the hub of government, from where a short walk across St James's Park leads to Buckingham Palace. Further west is Kensington and Hyde Park. Just north of the park is a popular hotel location, while to the south lie three of London's world-famous museums. A little further south-west is fashionable Chelsea.

Due east from Trafalgar Square, past Covent Garden, is the original City of London. This is both London's modern financial district and its ancient heart, where Roman walls butt up against skyscraping offices. Most visitors venture no further east than the Tower of London, but beyond here the new Docklands area is extending the sightseeing range. Finally, don't forget the south bank of the river, where the new Riverside Walk stretches from the South Bank Arts Centre to historic Southwark.

## What to See in Central London

### APSLEY HOUSE ⭐⭐

Apsley House, also known as the Wellington Museum, was the London home of Arthur Wellesley, first Duke of Wellington, from 1829 until his death in 1852. Wellington was the greatest soldier of his day, achieving major military successes in India, Spain and Portugal before crowning his career with the defeat of Napoleon at Waterloo in 1815.

The museum divides broadly into two parts. There are collections of plate and china, magnificent table centre-pieces, swords, medals and so on which relate to the Duke's adventures, and there is also an outstanding picture collection with paintings by many famous Old Masters. Intriguingly, the most memorable piece is an heroic oversized statue of Napoleon (commissioned by the Little Emperor and executed by Canova) in which he is depicted as a god. Prophetically, the figure of Victory in Napoleon's right hand is flying away from him.

- 28B2
- 149 Piccadilly, Hyde Park Corner
- 0171-499 5676
- Tue–Sun 11–5 (last admission 4:30). Closed Mon (open bank hol Mon except May Day), Good Fri, 24–26 Dec, 1 Jan
- The Grenadier(£)
- Hyde Park Corner
- Limited access due to steps
- Moderate. Open free on Waterloo Day (18 Jun)

### BANK OF ENGLAND MUSEUM ⭐

The Bank of England is the nation's central bank, functioning at the heart of one of the world's largest and most sophisticated financial centres. A visit to this small but lively museum will enlighten you as to its workings and its history. Highlights are its real gold bullion (each house-brick-sized bar is worth around £70,000), the repro-duction banking hall and the award-winning interactive screens and currency-dealing computer game.

- 29F3
- Bartholomew Lane
- 0171-601 5545 (recorded information)
- Mon–Fri 10–5. Closed public hols
- Sweetings (££)
- Bank
- Excellent
- Free

*The distinctive pink tailcoat uniform of the Bank of England's doormen dates back to 1684*

## BANQUETING HOUSE ✪

The Banqueting House is the only surviving part of Henry VIII's great Whitehall Palace, which burned down in 1698. Designed in classical style by Inigo Jones, it was completed in 1622 and is famous for its magnificent ceiling painting by Rubens. This huge work was commissioned by Charles I to celebrate the wisdom of the reign of the Stuart dynasty and depicts his father, James I. It was therefore to provide an ironic backdrop to the events of 30 January 1649 when Charles, defeated in the English Civil War, stepped out from a window of the Banqueting House on to a scaffold to face the executioner's axe.

The vaulted undercroft, formerly the wine cellar of James I, is also open to the public.

✚ 29D2
✉ Whitehall
☎ 0171-930 4179
🕐 Mon–Fri 10–5. Closed 24–26 Dec, 1 Jan, Good Fri, all public hols
🍴 Café-in-the-Crypt, St Martin-in-the-Fields, Trafalgar Square (£)
🚇 Westminster, Embankment
♿ Only undercroft accessible
💷 Moderate

## BBC EXPERIENCE ✪

If you have ever wondered just what went on behind the scenes at the British Broadcasting Corporation, here is your chance to find out. Most of the guided tour looks at great moments in recent British history from the perspective of the 'Beeb', which was born in London in 1922. However, the most satisfying aspects are those where the visitors are personally involved. You can take part in a three-minute radio play (either as an actor or as a sound-effects controller), read the weather, direct the camera action, experiment on a sound desk, be interviewed on Desert Island Discs or play with umpteen other clever hands-on television- and radio-related stations. One for BBC fans rather than casual overseas visitors.

✚ 28C3
✉ Broadcasting House (side entrance), Portland Place
☎ 0870-603 0304
🕐 Mon 1–4:30, Tue–Fri 9:45–4:30, Sat, Sun 9:45–5:30 (last tour).
🍴 BBC Café (£)
🚇 Oxford Circus, Great Portland Street
♿ All areas accessible
💷 Expensive
❓ Not suitable for children under seven

## BRITISH MUSEUM (► 16–17, TOP TEN)

Above: *opulent styling in the Banqueting House*

+ 28C2

☒ The Mall
☎ 0171-839 1377
recorded information
0171-799 2331(24hr)

**State Rooms**

☒ Buckingham Palace
🕐 Daily 9:30–4:30 second
week Aug–end Sep
🚇 Green Park, Hyde Park
Corner, St James's Park,
Victoria
♿ Excellent
💷 Very expensive

**Queen's Gallery**

☒ Buckingham Palace Road
🕐 Daily 9:30–4:30. Closed
Good Fri, 25–26 Dec
🚇 Victoria, Hyde Park
Corner, St James's Park
♿ Unsuitable for
wheelchairs
💷 Moderate

**Royal Mews**

☒ Buckingham Palace Road
🕐 12–4. Oct–Mar Wed only;
Mar–early Aug Tue–Thu;
early Aug–Sep Mon–Thu
🚇 Hyde Park Corner, St
James's Park, Victoria
♿ Excellent
💷 Moderate

Above: *Queen Victoria
Memorial and
Buckingham Palace*

### BUCKINGHAM PALACE ✪✪✪

World-famous as the London home of the Queen, this vast, sprawling, 600-room house was built mostly between 1820 and 1837, although the familiar East Front public face of the palace was not added until 1913. Buckingham Palace has been opening its doors to the public since 1993, with proceeds going towards the restoration of Windsor Castle (▶ 90). Visitors get to view 18 **State Rooms**, which are furnished with some of the most important works of art from the Royal Collection (including pictures by Van Dyck, Rembrandt and Rubens) – one of the largest and most valuable private art collections in the world. There's no chance of spotting any of the royal family, however, as they are always away at another of the royal residences when the palace is open.

If you miss the summer opening period you will have to content yourself with visiting the **Queen's Gallery**, which displays a relatively small changing exhibition drawn from the Royal Collection. More regal is the **Royal Mews**, where, among the horses and tack, is a display of the opulent carriages that are wheeled out on state occasions.

The colourful Changing of the Guard is still the most popular reason for visiting the palace. It takes places daily from April to July and on alternate days the rest of the year (wet weather permitting). At around 11:15 the St James's Palace part of the old guard marches down the Mall to meet the old guard of Buckingham Palace. There they await the arrival, at 11:30, of the new guard from Wellington Barracks who are accompanied by a band. Keys are ceremonially handed from the old to the new guard while the band plays. When the sentries have been changed, at around 12:05, the old guard return to Wellington Barracks and the new part of the St James's Palace guard march off to St James's Palace. As it can be extremely busy, aim to get close to the railings well before 11:00, particularly in high summer.

## CABINET WAR ROOMS ⭐⭐

This underground warren of rooms provided secure accommodation for the War Cabinet and their military advisers during World War II and was used on over 100 occasions. Today it is a time capsule, with the clocks stopped at 16:58 on 15 October 1940 and the ghost of Winston Churchill hanging heavy in the stuffy air. He slept in his underground office-cum-bedroom on just three occasions, but many of his stirring speeches to the nation were made from here and some of these are played to heighten the evocative atmosphere.

➕ 29D2
✉ Clive Steps, King Charles Street
☎ 0171-930 6961
🕐 Daily Apr–Sep 9:30–5:15, Oct–Mar 10–5:15
🚇 Westminster
♿ Excellent
🎟 Moderate
❓ Free audio guide

## CHELSEA ⭐⭐⭐

One of London's most fashionable suburbs in every sense, Chelsea was synonymous with both London's 'Swinging 60s' and the late 1970s punk rock movement. The latter was in fact born here, just off the famous King's Road. Today it is more up-market though still very lively. The area is best explored on foot (▶ 36).

➕ 28A1

*Chelsea's famous pink Albert Bridge is the prettiest of all the Thames crossings*

# Around Chelsea

**Distance**
5–6km (3–3¾ miles)

**Time**
2–6 hours depending on visits

**Start point**
📍 Sloane Square
➕ 28B1

**End point**
📍 Sloane Square
➕ 28B1

**Lunch**
Pizza Express (£)
✉ 152 King's Road
☎ 0171-351 5031

**Royal Hospital, Chelsea**
☎ 0171-730 0161
🕐 Mon–Sat 10–12, 2–4,
Sun 2–4
💷 Free

**Chelsea Physic Garden**
☎ 0171-352 5646
🕐 Early Apr–late Oct Wed
12–5, Sun 2–6
💷 Moderate

Start from Sloane Square underground station and walk straight ahead, down the King's Road, with Sloane Square and its statue of Sir Hans Sloane on your right.

*About 100m past the square turn left into Cheltenham Terrace with the Duke of York's (Territorial Army) Headquarters to your left. Turn right on to St Leonard's Terrace, former home of Bram Stoker (the creator of Dracula), with the green fields of Burton Court to your left.*

The building on the other side of the fields is the Royal Hospital, home to the famous Chelsea pensioners.

*Turn right into Royal Hospital Road (or left to visit the Hospital), passing the National Army Museum (▶ 59). Turn right into Tite Street, which includes such colourful former residents as Oscar Wilde (No 34), John Singer Sargent (No 31) and Augustus John (No 33). Turn right into Dilke Street, catching a glimpse through the side gate of the Chelsea Physic Garden.*

Physic simply meant 'of things natural'. This is the second-oldest botanic garden in the country, founded in 1673.

*Turn left into Swan Walk past the Physic Garden entrance, then right on to Cheyne Walk.*

This handsome terrace was also home to some of Chelsea's famous artists and writers including George Eliot (No 4) and Dante Gabrielle Rossetti (No 16).

*Continue along the Embankment, past pretty pink Albert Bridge, to Chelsea Old Church.*

A statue of Sir Thomas More sits outside the church and his intended tomb, inside, is occupied by his wife.

*Turn right into Church Street until you rejoin the shops of King's Road, then turn right to return to Sloane Square.*

### COMMONWEALTH EXPERIENCE ✪

The British Commonwealth is a legacy of Empire, comprising an association of 54 sovereign states that are, or at some time have been, ruled by Britain. They range from all over Africa to the Caribbean, Canada, Southeast Asia and the Pacific. The exhibition is set out in the fashion of a world trade fair, with 'stands' allocated to each state where various aspects of their respective cultures, arts and crafts are explored. Although most displays are old-fashioned they are usually attractive because of the colour and diversity of the subject matter and relief is provided by various hands-on exhibits. Bang up-to-date are Heliride, a simulated helicopter flight over Malaysia, and a new interactive gallery that demonstrates natural phenomena.

🔲 84C3
✉ Kensington High Street
☎ 0171-371 3530
🕐 Daily 10–5 (last admission 4:30). Closed week before Christmas to 26 Dec
🍴 Café (£)
🚇 High Street Kensington
♿ Excellent
🎫 Moderate

*It's not the quantity but the quality that counts at Courtauld Gallery*

### COURTAULD GALLERY ✪✪✪

The Courtauld Gallery has been called the greatest concentration of Western European art anywhere in the world and features a great collection of Impressionist paintings. It is housed in Somerset House, one of the finest and most important 18th-century public buildings in London.

The Impressionists and Post-Impressionists are top priority, particularly Van Gogh's *Self Portrait with Bandaged Ear* and Manet's *Bar at the Folies Bergère*. Other paintings include *Le Déjeuner sur l'Herbe*, also by Manet, *The Card Players* by Cézanne, *La Loge* by Renoir, *Two Dancers on a Stage* by Degas and Gauguin's Tahitian works. The collection goes back to the 15th century, and early masterpieces include works by Cranach the Elder, a superb Holy Trinity by Botticelli and from the early 17th century a large number of paintings by Rubens. There are also some fine 20th-century works.

🔲 29D3
✉ Somerset House, Strand
☎ 0171-873 2526
🕐 Mon–Sat 10–6, Sun 2–6
🍴 Café (£)
🚇 Temple (closed Sun), Covent Garden
♿ Good
🎫 Moderate

### COVENT GARDEN PIAZZA (► 18, TOP TEN)

# Around Covent Garden

**Distance**
3–4km (2½ miles)

**Time**
1 hour without stops

**Start point**
🚇 Leicester Square
➕ 29D3

**End point**
🚇 Covent Garden
➕ 29D3

**Lunch**
Neal's Yard Bakery
✉ Neal's Yard (£)
☎ 0171-836 5199

This walk can take all day if the shops and cafés along the way prove irresistible.

*Leave Leicester Square underground station via a Charing Cross Road exit and walk a short way in the direction of Trafalgar Square. Turn left into Cecil Court.*

While away some time here in one of London's most popular book-browsing alleyways, full of fascinating and individual small shops.

*At the top, cross St Martin's Lane and enter the tiny gas-lit alleyway marked Goodwin's Court (between Espresso and Cheque Point).*

This is the oldest residential part of Covent Garden with beautiful 18th-century bow-windowed houses.

*Turn left into Bedfordbury, then almost immediately right into New Row, a charming pedestrianised street with many excellent small shops. Continue up New Row to King Street, pausing to admire No 43, built in 1717, which is one of the oldest and most attractive buildings in the area.*

Almost opposite here is one of the entrances to St Paul's Church (► 18).

*Keep the Piazza and central market area (► 18) on your right and turn left into James Street, past Covent Garden underground station. Cross Long Acre into Neal Street, another of Covent Garden"s characterful pedestrianised shopping streets. Turn left into Short's Gardens, then, by the splendid water clock on top of the Neal's Yard Wholefood Warehouse, turn right into Neal's Yard.*

*The Neal's Yard water clock is typical of Covent Garden's creative and fun mood*

This delightfully pretty courtyard festooned with window boxes is a wholefood haven, full of vegetarian cafés and restaurants.

*Retrace your steps back to Covent Garden underground station.*

## DESIGN MUSEUM ✪✪

The Design Museum was set up in 1989 as the brainchild of Britain's leading design and style guru, Sir Terence Conran. Its aim is to promote an awareness of the importance of design and the contribution it makes to everyday life, particularly when related to mass-produced objects. Although this may not sound particularly promising (and the severe lines of its brilliant white Bauhaus building hardly provide reassurance to the casual visitor), it is well worth a visit. The collection divides broadly into two parts. The more conventional historic part shows the design evolution of familiar workaday items, such as domestic appliances, cameras and cars. The upper Review Gallery is an intriguing fly-on-the-wall showcase for the very latest ideas; some currently in production, some at prototype stage, others stuck permanently on the drawing board. Interactive computer stations cater for a new generation of would-be designers.

✚ 85D3
✉ Butler's Wharf, Shad Thames
☎ 0171-403 6933
🕐 Mon–Fri 11:30–6, Sat–Sun 12–6. Closed 25–26 Dec
🍴 Blueprint Café restaurant (££), café (£)
🚇 London Bridge, Tower Hill
♿ Excellent
💷 Moderate/expensive

## DICKENS HOUSE MUSEUM ✪✪

Dating from 1801, this smart middle-class residence is the only surviving house in which Charles Dickens lived for any length of time whilst in London. He stayed here from April 1837 to December 1839, long enough to secure his burgeoning reputation by writing the final instalments of *The Pickwick Papers*, almost all of *Oliver Twist*, the whole of *Nicholas Nickleby* and the start of *Barnaby Rudge*. Opened as a museum in 1925, the house how holds the finest collection of Dickens memorabilia in existence, with many of the exhibits reflecting the novels that were written here.

✚ 29D4
✉ 48 Doughty Street
☎ 0171-405 2127
🕐 Mon–Sat 10–5 (last admission 4:30). Closed Sun
🍴 October Gallery Café (£)
🚇 Russell Square, Chancery Lane (closed Sun)
♿ None
💷 Moderate

*48 Doughty Street, the birthplace of Oliver Twist, Fagin and a host of other great Dickens characters*

39

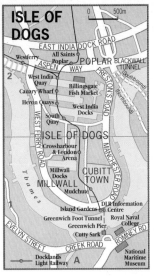

### DOCKLANDS ✪✪✪

London's Docklands stretch some 8km (5 miles) east of the Tower of London to the old Royal Docks. Historically, this area was the powerhouse of the Empire, at its height the busiest port in the world. It reached the peak of its activity in 1964 but changes in technology (most notably containerisation) signalled its sudden demise. Within a decade most of the quays and great swathes of nearby land were derelict and remained so until the early 1980s when the government began the world's largest urban redevelopment project to date. The transformation of this brave new boomtown has generated enormous controversy, with fortunes made and lost and completion still a long way off.

The centrepiece is Canary Wharf, Britain's tallest building at 243m. Often criticised for its communications infrastructure and relative isolation (though Canary Wharf is a mere 6km (3¾ miles) from the Bank of England), Docklands will receive a huge boost with the extension of the Jubilee underground line connecting it directly to Westminster.

# Around Docklands

St Katharine's Dock (► 68) marks the start of London's Docklands. The area goes to sleep at the weekends, so it is best to do this walk on a weekday.

*Follow St Katharine's Way along the river to Wapping High Street.*

The old warehouses along here which once held spices and tropical hardwoods have been converted into expensive apartments. At Wapping Pier Head some splendid Georgian houses, once the homes of wealthy wharf owners, can be seen. Beyond Waterside Gardens look at the handsome baroque Church of St George-in-the-East.

*If it is pub opening time (after 11:30am or 12 on Sunday) continue on to the atmospheric old Prospect of Whitby pub (► 97). From here retrace your steps a short way along Wapping Wall, turn right into Garnet Street, cross the main street known as The Highway and turn left then immediately right into Dellow Street, which leads to Shadwell Docklands Light Railway (DLR) station. Board the train for Island Gardens.*

You will soon enjoy great views from the high-level track down on to the incredible post-modernist developments that have taken place, and are still in progress, here in the centre of Docklands.

*Alight at Island Gardens.*

Admire the wonderful view across to Greenwich (► 82–3), and pick up the free map, Visiting Docklands on DLR, from the DLR information centre.

*Reboard the train and get off at Canary Wharf station.*

This is the business and leisure focal point of the new Docklands, with various places to eat, drink and shop.

*Take a stroll around its redeveloped docks, then either catch the DLR back to Tower Gateway or hop on the underground.*

**Distance**
Walk approximately 3km (1¾ miles)

**Time**
3–4 hours (walk and DLR), including stops

**Start point**
St Katharine's Dock
Tower Hill
✚ 85D3

**End point**
Canary Wharf
✚ 40A2

**Lunch**
Prospect of Whitby (£) or various options at Canary Wharf
✉ 57 Wapping Wall
☎ 0171-481 1095

Left: *Canary Wharf*
Below: *Docklands Light Railway*

## Dr Johnson's House

- ✠ 29E3
- ✉ 17 Gough Square
- ☎ 0171-353 3745
- 🕐 Mon–Sat 11–5:30
  (Oct–Apr 11–5)
- 🍴 Ye OldeCheshire
  Cheese (£)
- 🚇 Temple, Blackfriars
- ♿ Not suitable for
  wheelchair access
- 💷 Cheap/moderate

---

- ✠ 29F3
- ✉ Guildhall
- ☎ 0171-606 3030 (ext
  1450)
- 🕐 All areas May–Sep daily
  10–4, Oct–Apr
  Mon–Sat 10–4. Great
  hall and crypt (pre-
  booked tours only)
  occasionally closed when
  in use. Closed 24–25
  Dec, 1 Jan
- 🍴 The Place Below (£), St
  Mary-le-Bow Church,
  Cheapside
- 🚇 Bank, St Paul's
- ♿ Excellent
- 💷 Free
- ❓ Tours by arrangement

### FLEET STREET ✪

Fleet Street became the original publishing centre of London in 1500, when England's first press was set up here. From 1702 up to the 1980s it was also the home of England's newspapers until new technology meant they could decamp to cheaper, more efficient offices away from the Street of Ink. Today it is still worth a visit for St Bride's Church (▶ 65) and the little alleyways which run north of here. Wine Office Court is home to Ye Olde Cheshire Cheese, while close by is **Dr Johnson's House**, built c1700 and now a museum dedicated to the writer who gave us the first English dictionary.

### GUILDHALL ✪

The City of London has been governed from this site for over 800 years and the majestic centrepiece of the great hall dates back to 1430. Its huge crypt is even older, dating from the mid-13th century. The banners and stained-glass coats of arms that decorate the hall belong to the City Livery companies, formed in medieval times to represent and support their professions, and still in existence today. The Guildhall still holds various annual ceremonies, including the election of the Lord Mayor and the Lord Mayor's Banquet. Within the complex is a Clock Museum and the Guildhall Art Gallery (to be opened in 1999).

*Above: Dr Johnson, a great London wit*

*Left: the mythical British giant, Magog, at the Guildhall*

## HAMPSTEAD ⚫⚫⚫

Leafy Hampstead, London's most famous 'village', was developed as a spa in the 18th century and became a fashionable and exclusive retreat favoured by many prominent writers and artists. Spotting name plaques among the many beautiful former homes of luminaries such as Lord Byron, John Keats, H G Wells, Robert Louis Stephenson, D H Lawrence, John Constable and the like is a favourite visitor pastime. The steep narrow streets around the centre are very well preserved and retain an intimate feel. The most appealing include Flask Walk, Well Walk (where you'll find the original spa fountain), Holly Walk, Hampstead Grove and Church Row. Meanwhile, Hampstead High Street and Heath Street bristle with trendy restaurants, cafés and a good variety of small independent shops that cater for the well-heeled residents.

There are a number of low-key sights in the centre. **Burgh House** acts as a local museum; **Fenton House**, built in 1693, holds ceramics and a renowned collection of historic keyboard instruments; **Keats' House**, where the poet John Keats lived for almost two years, was closed for long-term repairs at the time of writing. Just south of here is the **Freud Museum**, where Sigmund Freud lived from 1938 until his death in 1939.

Hampstead's other claim to fame is Hampstead Heath, London's largest and most famous heathland covering some 324ha. One of north London's favourite summer walking spots, its ponds are also used for swimming. Parliament Hill is a traditional Sunday venue for kite-flying and offers great views across to central London. Much of the heath consists of undeveloped woodland, the main exception being the landscaped grounds of Kenwood House (➤ 50).

### Hampstead
✚ 84C4
🚇 Hampstead

### Tourist Information
✉ By the lido, southernmost point of the heath
🕐 Wed–Sun 10–12, 1–5

### Burgh House
✉ New End Square
☎ 0171-431 2516
🕐 Wed–Sun 12–5
💷 Free

### Fenton House
✉ Windmill Hill
☎ 0171-435 3471
🕐 Mar Sat–Sun 2–5;
Apr–Oct Sat–Sun, bank hol Mon 11–5:30, Wed–Fri 2–5:30. Closed Sat and Nov–Feb
💷 Moderate

### Keats' House
✉ Keats Grove
☎ 0171-435 2062
🕐 Closed for major repairs, phone for details
💷 Phone for details

### Freud Museum
✉ 20 Maresfield Gardens
☎ 0171-435 2002
🕐 Wed–Sun 12–5
🚇 Finchley Road
💷 Cheap/moderate

Left: *The Holly Bush is a favourite Hampstead hideaway*

*Harrod's Food Halls, a shrine to gourmets and foodies*

### HARRODS

Harrods is much more than just a shop, it is an internationally famous institution and even the most reluctant shopper should venture into its cathedral-like portals. The store began trading here in 1849 as a small, family-run grocery shop and by 1905 the present magnificent terracotta building was complete. With a selling area of over 10ha and some 330 departments, it is Britain's biggest department store.

Among the highlights are the lavish and stylish Food Halls. The Meat Hall is gloriously decorated with 1902 tiles, while the centrepiece fresh-fish display is an extravaganza of the bounty of the sea.

### HMS BELFAST

HMS *Belfast* is Europe's last surviving big warship from World War II and occupies a spectacular permanent mooring site on the Thames just upstream from Tower Bridge, opposite Southwark Crown Court. Launched in 1938, she saw action in the Arctic, at the D-Day Normandy landings and in the Korean War from 1950 to 1952, before being decommissioned.

Today her seven cramped labyrinthine decks, which once accommodated a crew of up to 800 men, serve as a museum, giving landlubbers a salty flavour of the rigours of serving at sea. The bridge, galley, operations room, punishment cells, engine and boiler rooms can all be explored. There are also various naval displays.

+ 28B2
✉ Brompton Road
☎ 0171-730 1234
⏰ Mon, Tue, Sat 10–6, Wed–Fri 10–7
🍴 Variety in store(£–£££)
Ⓠ Knightsbridge
♿ Good
❓ No one admitted wearing scruffy clothes, vests, shorts or backpacks

+ 29F3
✉ Morgan's Lane, off Tooley Street
☎ 0171-407 6434
⏰ Daily: summer 10–6, winter 10–5. Closed 24–26 Dec
🍴 Café(£)
Ⓠ London Bridge, Tower Hill. Ferry from Tower Hill pier in summer
♿ Not suitable for wheelchair visitors
 Moderate

---

> ## *Did you know ?*
>
> *The most famous Highgate epitaph belongs to Karl Marx – 'Workers of All Lands Unite' – though the most diffident belongs to comedian Max Wall – '... the most I've had is just a talent to amuse'. Carved on the tomb of Tom Sayers, last of the great British bare-fisted boxers, is the huge effigy of his faithful dog, the chief mourner among 10,000 people at the funeral.*

## HIGHGATE ●●●

The charming village of Highgate lies just east of Hampstead Heath and like its famous neighbour, Hampstead (► 43), was a favourite retreat for the upper classes and literary figures, including Samuel Taylor Coleridge (author of *The Rime of the Ancient Mariner*).

Its unlikely, though perennially popular, visitor highlight is Highgate Cemetery. Opened in 1839, the cemetery soon became the fashionable final resting place of politicians, poets, actors and other Victorian personalities. Monuments grew ever larger and more ornate and Highgate Cemetery soon turned into a tourist attraction. The atmospheric West Cemetery is the real draw, piled high with crumbling catacombs, Egyptian columns and obelisks, ivy-clad vaults and grand mausoleums. It looks like the set for a Hammer horror movie and is said to have inspired Bram Stoker (the author of *Frankenstein*). However, the most famous personalities are buried in the East Cemetery and include Karl Marx, Sir Ralph Richardson, Mary Ann Evans (pen-name George Eliot) and comedian Max Wall.

## HOUSES OF PARLIAMENT (► 19, TOP TEN)

## HYDE PARK ●

The largest and most famous of central London's open spaces, Hyde Park covers around 138ha and was once the royal hunting ground of Henry VIII and Elizabeth I. It was first opened to the public by James I. Bounded by Park Lane, Bayswater Road and Knightsbridge, its western extension is Kensington Gardens (► 49).

At its northeast corner, at the very end of Oxford Street, is Marble Arch; it was originally erected in front of Buckingham Palace but moved as a result of palace redevelopment. Near by is Speakers' Corner, London's most famous 'soapbox' where anyone may air their views (within reason).

Flowing through the park is the Serpentine lake, created in 1730, and just west of here is the **Serpentine Gallery**, featuring revolving exhibitions of contemporary art.

---

✚ 84C5
✉ Swain's Lane
☎ 0181-340 1834
🕐 East Cemetery open daily 10–4, Sat, Sun 11–4. West Cemetery, admission by tour only; Sat–Sun 11–4 each hour, Mon–Fri tours at 12, 2, 4. Nov–Feb tours at weekends only
🍴 Café Mozart, 17 Swain's Lane (£)
🚇 Highgate/Archway
♿ The East Cemetery is nearly all freely accessible. The West is partly accessible
🎟 East Cemetery cheap, West Cemetery moderate.
❓ No children under eight in West Cemetery

---

✚ 28B2
🕐 Daily at any time
🍴 The Orangery (££), Kensington Gardens
🎟 free
🚇 Marble Arch, Knightsbridge

**Serpentine Gallery**
☎ 0171-402 6075
🕐 10–6 daily during exhibitions
♿ Serpentine Gallery totally accessible
🎟 free
🚇 Lancaster Gate

🕂 29B2

✉ Lambeth Road

☎ 0171-416 5000. Recorded information ☎ 0891-600 140

🕐 Daily 10–6. Closed 24–26 Dec

🍴 Café (£), picnic room open weekends, school hols

🚇 Lambeth North, Elephant & Castle, Waterloo

♿ Excellent

🎟 Moderate (free after 4:30)

*The Imperial War Museum's big naval guns could once fire an 875kg shell a distance of 30km!*

## IMPERIAL WAR MUSEUM ✪✪✪

Dedicated to telling the story of world conflict during the 20th century, the Imperial War Museum has the most impressive entrance of any London museum. Suspended from the ceiling of its glass atrium and occupying two floors around the atrium are World War II fighter planes, biplanes from the Great War, a V2 rocket, a Polaris missile, field guns, tanks, submarines, plus over 40 other large exhibits. Despite this grand martial entrance, however (which children revel in), this is a thought-provoking, sometimes heart-rending museum, which tells the story of war dispassionately, often from the point of view of the ordinary soldier or the folks left at home. The emphasis inevitably is on the two World Wars and each has a large walk-in section where you can experience the horrors of the trenches and the claustrophobia of an air-raid shelter, then the aftermath of a bombing raid.

The narrative collection is brilliantly chosen, comprising many personal and almost everyday objects from the trenches, the concentration camps, the Far East, the Eastern Front, the Atlantic Ocean and every other significant theatre of war. These are combined with memorabilia such as recruiting posters, dramatic contemporary film footage and – best of all – spoken first-hand accounts from ordinary combatants and survivors.

Conflicts since 1945 are also well handled and the Secret War Exhibition, detailing clandestine operations from World War I to the present day, is fascinating. The top floor is dedicated to war artists and features many highly acclaimed works.

# Around the Inns of Court

This walk should be done on a weekday as the nearest underground stations are closed on Sundays and several areas within the Inns are closed at the weekend.

*Turn left out of Temple underground station, go up the steps and turn right into Temple Place, which leads (via a car park entrance) to Inner Temple. Turn left up the steps to Fountain Court.*

The splendid Elizabethan hall and the adjacent gardens are occasionally open.

*Continue straight on beneath the archway following the sign to Lamb's Buildings into Middle Temple. Go up the steps to the left of the building ahead to find Temple Church, famous for its effigies of 13th-century Crusader knights. Leave Temple by the alleyway adjacent to Dr Johnson's Buildings.*

At the end is the doorway to Prince Henry's Room, a rare Elizabethan survivor with a fine 17th-century interior.

*Cross Fleet Street, turn left and then right alongside the monumental Royal Courts of Justice into Bell Yard. At the end of Bell Yard turn left and, by Legastat printers, turn right into New Square, the heart of Lincoln's Inn.*

Lincoln's Inn's splendid hall (to the left) isn't open but you can visit the chapel (to the right), built in 1620.

*Continue through the Inn and exit right at the corner of Stone Buildings. Cross Chancery Lane, turn right, then go left into Southampton Buildings, which leads to Staple Inn.*

This is a former Inn of Chancery (a prep school for the Inns of Court); note its Elizabethan façade on High Holborn.

*Cross High Holborn, turn left, then, by the Cittie of York pub, go right into Gray's Inn. Duck beneath the arch to the left of the hall (closed) to Gray's Inn Gardens. Return to High Holborn for Chancery Lane tube.*

**Distance**
Approximately 4km (2½ miles)

**Time**
2–3 hours depending on visits

**Start point**
🚇 Temple (closed Sun)
✚ 29D3

**End point**
🚇 Chancery Lane (closed Sun)
✚ 29D4

**Lunch**
Cittie of York, Holborn (£) or picnic in Gray's Inn Gardens

**Middle Temple Hall**
🕐 Mon–Fri 10–12, 3–4

**Middle Temple Gardens**
🕐 May–Jul, Sep
Mon–Fri 12–3

**Prince Henry's Room**
✉ 17 Fleet Street
🕐 Mon–Sat 11–2

🛈 All Free

*The Temple Church, built in 1185*

### INNS OF COURT ✪✪✪

The Inns of Court, the training grounds for the country's barristers, date from medieval times. Today there are just four surviving: Inner Temple, Middle Temple, Lincoln's Inn and Gray's. Each resembles a small college campus, with a library, chapel, hall and barristers' chambers. Their grounds, usually open to the public from Monday to Friday, are central London's most charming and peaceful oases, and their narrow alleyways and small courtyards, many still gaslit, are very atmospheric in the early evening (➤ 47).

### JERMYN STREET ✪✪

Jermyn (pronounced German) Street is a slice of traditional 'Gentleman's London', famous for its exclusive and elegant shops. Cigar smokers should look in at Davidoff, while pipe smokers will enjoy Dunhill, whose shop also holds an intriguing **Pipe Smokers' Museum**. Don't miss Floris (at No 89), Paxton & Whitfield (No 93) and Bates (No 21a).

### JEWEL TOWER ✪

This venerable, solitary tower is one of the few remaining parts of the old Palace of Westminster (➤ 19). Built in 1366, it was used to house the personal valuables of Edward III and was known as the Royal Wardrobe. Today it makes an excellent introduction to the Houses of Parliament with an exhibition about their history and procedural practices. You can also take a 'tour' of Parliament on a multimedia touch-screen machine.

➕ 29D3
🚇 Green Park, Piccadilly Circus
♿ None
✋ Free

**Pipe Smokers' Museum**
➕ 28C3
✉ Alfred Dunhill, Duke Street
☎ 0171-838 8000
🕐 Mon–Sat 10–4
✋ Free

➕ 29D2
✉ Old Palace Yard
☎ 0171-222 2219
🕐 Daily. Apr–Oct 10–1, 2–6 (6PM/dusk Oct), Nov–Mar 10–1, 2–4
🍴 Café-in-the-Crypt (£)
🚇 Westminster
♿ None
✋ Cheap

*The Jewel Tower once held the king's jewels, furs, clothes and gold vessels*

## KENSINGTON PALACE AND KENSINGTON GARDENS ✪✪✪

William III was the first monarch to set up home in Kensington Palace, in 1689, and it was here in 1819 that the future Queen Victoria was born. Royal patronage continues with several members of the present royal family having palace apartments and in September 1997 it was a focus of the country's grief as the last home of the late Princess Diana. Thousands upon thousands of floral tributes were piled up in front of the palace gates in an unforgettable outpouring of emotion.

The fabric of the present palace, which actually resembles a country house in both style and size, dates largely from the early 18th century. The parts which are open to the visitor divide broadly into two areas: the State Apartments and the Court Dress Collection. The Apartments are striking for their magnificent ceiling paintings by William Kent and some impressive and curious *trompe-l'œil* effects. The Court Dress Collection, recently reorganised and refurbished, features a superb collection of court finery. Visitors are also guided through the elaborate process of what it was like to dress for court. Surrounding the palace are pretty sunken gardens and a red-brick orangery, now a restaurant.

Outside the palace gates is Kensington Gardens, which runs east into Hyde Park. This pretty lawned expanse boasts two famous statues. To the north is Peter Pan, and to the south is the amazingly intricate 53m-high Albert Memorial, dedicated to Prince Albert, Queen Victoria's much-loved consort.

✚ 84C3
✉ Kensington Gardens
☎ 0171-937 9561
🕐 Daily; phone for specific opening times
🍴 The Orangery (£–££)
Ⓜ High Street Kensington, Queensway
♿ Limited
💷 Expensive
❓ Guided tours

*The gates of Kensington Palace became a sad place of pilgrimage after the death of Princess Diana in 1997*

49

## KENWOOD HOUSE ★★

84C5
Hampstead Lane
0181-348 1286
Daily: Apr–Sep 10–6, Oct–Mar 10–4
Restaurant, café (£–££)
Hampstead
Good
Free (admission charge for exhibitions)

*Part of Adam's beautiful library in Kenwood House*

If you would like to see a real country house without leaving central London then Kenwood, on the north of Hampstead Heath (► 43), fits the bill perfectly. It was remodelled in 1764 by Robert Adam, whose signature pale blue, neo-classical design (made famous by Wedgwood pottery) is immediately apparent on entry to the house. The paintings at Kenwood are known as the Iveagh Bequest and form one of the most important collections bequeathed to the nation. They are mostly 17th- and 18th-century works from the English, Dutch and French schools, though recent additions include much earlier paintings by Botticelli and Hans Memling. The most

famous is a Rembrandt self-portrait, acknowledged as one of his very best. Also notable are works by Frans Hals and Vermeer. The architectural *tour de force* of the house is the library, with its elaborately decorated tunnel-vaulted ceiling and Corinthian columns. It is considered one of Adam's finest interiors.

The beautiful gardens at Kenwood are the most cultivated part of Hampstead Heath, with a lawned amphitheatre sloping down to a lake. During the summer this becomes London's finest al-fresco classical music venue – American visitors note, Handel's *Fireworks Music* is played every 4 July with accompanying pyrotechnics!

## LEIGHTON HOUSE ★★

84C3
12 Holland Park Road
0171-602 3316
Mon–Sat 11–5:30
Belvedere (£–££)
High Street Kensington
Not suitable for wheelchair users
Free
Guided tours; audio guides

The distinguished Victorian artist Frederic Lord Leighton (1830–96) created this beautiful romantic house between 1864 and 1866 and lived here until his death in 1896. The centrepiece is the Arab Hall, a glorious mini-Alhambra featuring a dome from Damascus, window screens from Cairo and Leighton's highly valued, rare collection of 15th- and 16th-century Islamic tiles from Cairo, Damascus and Rhodes. The other rooms are much more restrained but contain some fine works by Lord Leighton and his famous Pre-Raphaelite associates.

Left: *Lloyd's of London's space-age building.*
Below: *Lloyd's doormen in 17th-century colours*

## LLOYDS BUILDING ✪✪

Designed by Richard Rogers, of Georges Pompidou Center (Paris) fame, and sharing the same characteristic of wearing its guts on its sleeve, this stunning glass and steel tower ('a post-modern oil refinery' said one critic) was the most controversial building in England when finished in 1986. Sadly it is no longer open to the public but remains one of London's most potent architectural statements.

✚ 29F3
✉ Leadenhall Street
◷ Closed to public
🍴 Leadenhall Wine Bar (£), Leadenhall Market
🚇 Aldgate

## LONDON AQUARIUM ✪✪

This is the capital's first real aquarium and one of the new generation of maximum-visibility, large-tank, natural-atmosphere aquaria which are currently enjoying great popularity. The centrepiece is two giant 8m-high tanks featuring Atlantic and Pacific displays. The latter is home to sand tiger and brown sharks, and large rays that glide silently between giant, sunken, replica Easter Island statues. The Reef and Living Coral exhibit and the Indian Ocean tank boast the most colourful denizens of the deep, while the highlight for many children is the chance to stroke a stingray in the touch pool.

✚ 29D2
✉ County Hall Riverside Building, Westminster Bridge Road
☎ 0171-967 8000
◷ Daily 10–6
🍴 Global Café Bar (£), Four Regions Chinese Restaurant (£££)
🚇 Waterloo, Westminster
♿ Excellent
💷 Expensive

51

# In the Know

If you only have a short time to visit London, or would like to get a real flavour of the city, here are some ideas:

## 10

### Ways to Be a Local

**Read** *Time Out* for What's On and the *London Evening Standard*.

**Visit the South Kensington** museums for the last hour or so when admission is free.

**Shop at one** of the many street markets.

**Settle down** to watch a game of cricket on Kew Green.

**Take a historic** walking tour.

**Eat in one** of London's few surviving pie 'n' mash shops (➤ 96).

**Ride the top deck** of any regular London bus.

**Buy a sandwich** and eat it in one of London's parks, or if you're in the city, in a churchyard.

**Go to Speaker's Corner** on a Sunday morning.

**See the Changing of the Guard** at Horse Guards, Whitehall (➤ 77).

## 10

### Good Places to Have Lunch

**The Orangery (£–££)**
✉ Kensington Palace Gardens. Part-designed by Wren. Go for tea.

**Jasons (£££)**
✉ opposite 60 Blomfield Road, Maida Vale
☎ 0171-286 6752. Mauritian seafood in a beautiful canalside setting.

**The Ritz Hotel (£££)**
✉ 150 Piccadilly
☎ 0171-493 2687. Palatial luxury at a set price.

**The Belvedere (£–££)**
✉ Holland Park
☎ 0171-602 1238. Great views and a beautiful setting.

**Goddard's Ye Old Pie House**
✉ 45 Greewich Church Street, Greenwich. The best value meat pies in London.

**Neal's Yard Bakery (£)**
✉ Neal's Yard, Covent Garden ☎ 0171-836 5199. One of a choice of cheap wholefood eateries set in a charming courtyard.

**Odette's (£££)**
✉ 130 Regent's Park Road ☎ 0171-586 5486. Excellent food served in the garden in summer.

**China City (£)**
✉ White Bear Yard, 25a Lisle Street ☎ 0171-734 3388. For some of Chinatown's best *dim sum.*

**Prêt à Manger (£)**
For lunch on the move; good-quality fresh hand-made snacks and sandwiches. Branches all over central London.

**A London park (£–£££)**
Regent's Park, Greenwich Park, Hampstead Heath. Take a picnic.

*A typical London pub*

### Spaniards
 Spaniard's Road, Hampstead Heath. Bags of history and a lovely garden.
### Sun
 63 Lamb's Conduit Street. Small Bloomsbury boozer with a great choice of beers.
### Trafalgar Tavern
 5 Park Row, Greenwich. Perfect riverside location.
### Windsor Castle
 114 Campden Hill Road. A real 'country pub' in Notting Hill.
### Ye Grapes
 16 Shepherd Market. Typical Victorian pub in the centre of Mayfair.
### Ye Olde Cock Tavern
 22 Fleet Street. Classic City inn, once frequented by Pepys and Johnson.

---

## 10
## Best London Vantage Points

**St Paul's Cathedral** (► 22)
**Parliament Hill** (► 43)
**Westminster Cathedral Tower** (► 76)
**Oxo Tower** (► 63)
**Hilton Hotel, Hyde Park** (► 97 side panel)
**Tower Bridge** (► 74)
**The Monument** (► 56)
**The Great Balloon Experience** Get hauled up in a tethered balloon hundreds of feet above south London at Spring Gardens, Auckland Street ☎ 0345-023 842
**Greenwich Park**, Old Royal Observatory (► 83)
**Waterloo Bridge** (► 9)

Left: *eating alfresco*
Far left: *Petticoat Lane street market*

---

## 10
## Good Pubs

### Fox & Anchor
 115 Charterhouse Street. Atmospheric Smithfield market pub with unique opening hours to suit the workers (7AM– 9PM Monday to Friday).
### Grenadier
 Old Barrack Yard, Wilton Row. Fine 18th-century Knightsbridge mews pub.
### Red Lion
 Duke of York Street. Tiny St James's Victorian gin palace (closed Sundays).
### Salisbury
 90 St Martin's Lane. Bustling, beautifully preserved Victorian pub at the heart of Theatreland.

---

## 5
## Top Activities

**Windsurf** in Docklands at the Surrey Docks Watersport Centre. (☎ 0181-237 4009)
**Go horse riding** in Hyde Park (► 115).
**Row on the Thames** at Richmond (☎ 0181-948 8270).
**Indulge yourself** at The Sanctuary, Covent Garden (ladies only) – a wonderful, if expensive, health club (☎ 0171-420 5151).
**Ice skate** in the heart of the City at Broadgate Ice Rink from October to March (☎ 0171-505 4068).

29F2
Tooley Street
0171-403 0606 (recorded
information); 0171-403
7221 general enquiries
Daily: Apr–Sep 10–6:30,
Oct–Mar 10–5:30 (last
admission 1 hour before
closing). Closed 25 Dec
Café dell' Ugo, 56–8
Tooley Street (£–££)
London Bridge
Excellent
Very expensive

28B4
Marylebone Road
0171-935 6861
Mon–Fri 12:20–5,
Sat–Sun and school hols
10:20–5. Closed 25 Dec
Madame Tussaud's Café
(£)
Baker Street
Excellent
Expensive. Combined
discount ticket with
Madame Tussaud's
(▶ 56) available

*The green copper dome
of the London
Planetarium is a Baker
Street landmark*

29D3
Covent Garden
0171-836 8557 (recorded
information); 0171-379
6344 general enquiries
Daily 10–6 (Fri 11–6). Last
admission 5:15. Closed
24, 25 Dec
The Transport Café (£)
Covent Garden
Excellent
Moderate
Actors provide free daily
tours for young children,
also free guided tours at
weekends and bank hols

## LONDON DUNGEON

'Abandon hope all who enter here' is the message of the London Dungeon, the world's first and foremost museum of medieval (and other) horrors. It was begun in 1975 by a London housewife whose children were disappointed by the lack of blood and gore on display at the Tower of London. Certainly no one leaves the Dungeon with such complaints! Recently revamped to even scarier heights, the dark tunnels beneath London Bridge now include many more blood-curdling special effects, with a 'dark ride' (in every sense) and costumed actors to enhance the scream factor. Ghouls and the curious, including most of London's overseas teenagers, make this one of the capital's most visited attractions, but this is definitely not a place for young children or the faint of heart.

## LONDON PLANETARIUM

Connected to Madame Tussaud's, the Planetarium is devoted to the exploration of space. Star shows run every 40 minutes and entertaining, educational interactive exhibition areas keep visitors busy while waiting. The show (which changes periodically) is a hybrid of traditional planetarium star-gazing and 3-D space adventures using the latest in projection and simulator techniques.

## LONDON TRANSPORT MUSEUM

At first glance a museum of London Transport may not look terribly interesting, but if you want to wallow in a little London nostalgia or if you have children in tow you can easily spend an enjoyable couple of hours here. The mainstay of the collection is its handsome historical hardware – evocative old double-deckers, the earliest horse-drawn London buses, a steam-driven train that ran underground (and managed to consume its own smoke) and so on. However, it is also very much a hands-on museum, with lots of activities for children and adults. You can ring bells, clamber on vehicles and if you think you could have driven the bus or underground train as well as the driver who brought you here, then take the simulator controls and find out.

## LONDON ZOO ⊕⊕

Opened in 1828, this was the world's first serious zoo. It soon achieved worldwide fame and reached its peak in the 1950s, when visitor numbers topped over 3 million per year. In recent times, however, as a result of current opinion regarding captive animals and a new generation of open, cage-free zoos, attendances fell so dramatically that it too was put on the endangered list. Now, thankfully, its future is looking secure and even though too many of its cages and enclosures are still small and old-fashioned, it still makes an enjoyable family day out for most visitors.

The zoo is not overly large but it's best to plan your day around the timetable of activities, such as feeding times, talks, shows and the entertaining Animals in Action presentations. Other highlights include the Mappin Terrace sloth bears, the penguin pool, the Snowdon Aviary and the elephant house (particularly at weighing and bathing times).

### Did you know ?

*That it was London Zoo's very first elephant, named Jumbo (acquired in 1867) who gave his name to any object of giant size (such as the jumbo jet). The elephants were such a novelty that they became the talk of London and so frantic was the 'elephant-mania' that Jumbo's mate, Alice, lost some 30cm of her trunk to a ruthless souvenir hunter!*

✚ 84C4
✉ Regent's Park
☎ 0171-722 3333
🕐 Open daily; Mar–Oct 10–5:30, Nov–Feb 10–4 Last admission 1 hour before closing time Closed 25 Dec
🍴 Café-restaurant (£)
Ⓜ Camden Town
♿ Good
💲 Expensive/very expensive

Above: *The brutalist architecture of the Elephant House was designed to echo its occupant's rough skin*

### MADAME TUSSAUD'S ✪✪✪

The grand old dame of London tourism, Madame T's has for several years been the capital's top entrance-paid attraction, as infamous for its queues (which you can now avoid) as for the excellence of its lifelike figures. Madame Tussaud began her career making death masks of guillotine victims, moved to England in 1802 and set up in London in 1835. You can still see artefacts of the French Revolution, including the waxworks' oldest figure – Madame Dubarry (Louis XV's mistress), made in 1765. She is cast as The Sleeping Beauty, with an ingenious breathing mechanism to keep her slumbering eternally. Highlights are very much a personal thing, though you'll doubtless linger in the Garden Party area which features current popular celebrities.

The 200 Years exhibition explores Tussaud's fascinating history and remarkably little-changed techniques. The display of discarded heads of former waxworks is an illuminating barometer of who is in fashion and who has dropped from favour. The Grand Hall brings together politicians and royalty, while The Chamber of Horrors is more horrible than ever. Far better to whisk young children off on the enjoyable Disney-like Spirit of London ride, replete with animatronic figures and special effects.

✚ 28B4
✉ Marylebone Road
☎ 0171-935 6861
🕐 Mon–Fri 10–5:30, Sat–Sun 9:30–5:30. Opens earlier during school hols. Closed 25 Dec
🍴 Café (£)
🚇 Baker Street
♿ Superstars area and Spirit of London ride not accessible to wheelchairs
✋ Very expensive. Combined discount ticket with London Planetarium available
❓ To avoid waiting in line book in advance (for either or both attractions) by credit card,

*Above: Madame T's is a capital institution*

*Right: the Monument was once a favourite London suicide spot*

### MONUMENT ✪

The Monument is the world's highest free-standing column; it measures 62m, which is exactly the distance due east to the site of the bakery in Pudding Lane where the Great Fire of London began in 1666. It was commissioned by King Charles II 'to preserve the memory of this dreadful Visitation' and designed jointly by Christopher Wren and Robert Hooke. You can climb the inside of the column via a 311-step spiral staircase and enjoy views of the City.

✚ 29F3
✉ Monument Street
☎ 0171-626 2717
🕐 Apr–Sep Mon–Fri 9–5:40, Sat–Sun 2–5:40; Oct–Mar Mon–Sat 10–4:40
🍴 Leadenhall Wine Bar (£), Leadenhall Market
🚇 Monument
♿ No facilities
✋ Cheap

*The largest and best-preserved Roman mosaic in London and a reconstruction of a Roman kitchen, Museum of London*

## MUSEUM OF LONDON ●●●

Reputed to be the most comprehensive city museum in the world, the Museum of London tells you everything you ever wanted to know about the history of the capital. The displays are attractive and the captions punchy and entertaining. There's a lot to see, but you don't have to do it all at once as your admission ticket allows free re-entry within three months.

Displays are chronological, beginning with the Prehistoric Gallery then progressing to Roman London. The latter is a highlight, with reconstructed rooms and superb sculptures from the Temple of Mithras. Trot briskly from the Dark Ages to Stuart times. Here you will find Oliver Cromwell's death mask, the splendid Cheapside (jewellery) Hoard, plague exhibits and the Great Fire Experience, accompanied by a reading from the diary of Samuel Pepys.

The lower-level galleries, from late Stuart times to the present, feature many fascinating large-scale exhibits. Most handsome of all is the opulent Lord Mayor's State Coach, made in 1757. London's dark side is represented by the reconstructed Wellclose Square cell and part of the chilling Newgate Prison. Move on and cheer yourself up with the artistic achievements of the Great Exhibition of 1851.

Best of all for many visitors are the remaining galleries, Imperial Capital (with some excellent shop reconstructions), early 20th-century London (Selfridge's art deco lift is an unlikely but unmissable highlight) and World War II. London Now brings the story bang up to date.

🚇 29E3

✉ London Wall

☎ 0171-600 3699. Information line 0171-600 0807

🕐 Tue–Sat and bank hols 10–5:50, Sun 12–5:50. Last admission 5:30. Closed 24–26 Dec, 1 Jan

🍽 Good café-restaurant (£)

🚇 Barbican, St Paul's, Moorgate

♿ Excellent

🎟 Moderate. Entrance ticket valid for free return within three months. Free admission after 4:30

❓ Family events, including costumed actors, most Suns and during school hols

29D3

South Bank, Waterloo (next to Waterloo Bridge)

0171-401 2636 (24-hour information line)

Daily 10–6 (last admission 5). Closed 24–25 Dec

Film Café (£)

Waterloo, Embankment

Excellent, 0171–928 3535

Expensive

*This particular Statue of Liberty was a prop from the movie* Little Shop of Horrors

## MUSEUM OF THE MOVING IMAGE

Dedicated to the world of film and television, the award-winning Museum of the Moving Image (MOMI) may be one of London's newer collections but it is already well established as a favourite with visitors and Londoners alike. The history of moving images is covered in meticulous detail, from Javanese shadow puppets through all sorts of ingenious optical illusions to today's silver-screen technology. There's also a tremendous range of film memorabilia, from Charlie Chaplin's hat and cane to Marilyn Monroe's dresses, from a 1935 Frankenstein to *Star Wars* stormtroopers. The real fun of the museum, however, is its interactive aspect, with costumed actor-guides who happily accost visitors and throw themselves into their roles as film directors, ushers, casting crew, etc. You can audition for a Hollywood film, create your own cartoons, fly like Superman over London, be interviewed by Barry Norman, or read the news from an autocue. Less interactively inclined visitors can simply stare at the dozens of screens, wallowing in childhood television nostalgia, studying historic newsreels or thrilling to the classic films of the cinema.

*This superb mid-18th century Grenadier Officer's cap is one of many colourful uniforms on display at the National Army Museum*

## NATIONAL ARMY MUSEUM ⭐

The first professional British Army was formed in 1485 and this museum, housed in a concrete bunker, covers its history in the five centuries to date. Audio-visual presentations, dioramas and lifelike soldier mannequins bring to life the lot of the ordinary soldier in a manner that concentrates more on the daily hardships than on the glory of war.

Start in the basement, which moves from Agincourt to the American War of Independence. As well as a fine display of swords you can try on a civil war helmet and feel the weight of a cannon shot.

The Road to Waterloo follows the story of the soldiers in Wellington's army and includes a huge, scale model of the battlefield. Move on briskly through the Victorian Soldier exhibitions and, when you start to get fatigued by the uniforms and medals, pop up to the Uniform Gallery – not for more uniforms, but to learn some of the fascinating stories of the 'she-soldiers' of the 17th and 18th centuries who dressed as men in order to fight in the British Army. The Brixmis exhibition on information gathered during the Cold War is also surprisingly interesting.

Displays on the two World Wars bring the story up to date, though if you are particularly interested in this period you would be better off paying a visit to the Imperial War Museum (➤ 46).

28B1
Royal Hospital Road, Chelsea
0171-730 0717
Daily 10–5:30. Closed 24–26 Dec, 1 Jan, Good Fri, early May bank hol
Basic café (£)
Sloane Square
Excellent 0171-730 0717 ext 2243
Free

# Food & Drink

Long the butt of culinary jokes, the capital's restaurants and British cooking have improved so much in recent years that London is now regarded as among the best places in the world for eating out. The only drawback is that this can be expensive, but fixed-price meals, particularly at lunchtime, can make your pound go very much further.

**Ye Olde Cheshire Cheese**

Above: *grab lunch in Ye Olde Cheshire Cheese*
Below: *afternoon tea*

## What to Eat

The world is your oyster, with representatives from virtually every culinary school on the planet. The most acclaimed generally fall under the banner of Modern European cuisine. When in Britain, however, it would be a shame not to eat British food, from traditional hearty English dishes to the more sophisticated, foreign-influenced, eclectic Modern British cuisine. Long assimilated into mainstream British culture, Indian food should also be on your personal menu. And of course, at the end of the night look for the nearest fish and chip shop!

## Where to Eat

At the cutting edge of the market the current vogue is for restaurants to boast huge dining rooms, with some likened to ocean liners. Restaurant fashion seems almost as important as the food itself and many of London's leading eating houses are owned by renowned design guru Sir Terence Conran.

Fashion pervades all the way down the price scale, with yesterday's humble cafés making way for today's trendy caffés. In line with this trend, museum catering has improved enormously in the last few years, too.

If you're on a tight budget, are not concerned with frills, but want to avoid fast-food insipidity, you'll still be able to find one of London's myriad cheap and cheerful old-fashioned Italian family-run cafés.

## When, Where and What to Drink

London is no longer straitjacketed by antiquated licensing laws and, consequently, you can now drink alcohol at most times of the day or night. As with restaurants, there are any number of different styles of bar, many of the designer variety. These can be so expensive and so busy admiring their own reflection that it's a wonder they get any custom. London has many fine traditional English pubs serving traditional English beer. At its best, it is hand-drawn from oak casks and is usually darker and warmer than lager beers.

## British Food

There are places still serving the type of food Charles Dickens would recognise – hot savoury pies, roast meats and game, and to follow steamed sweet puddings and pies – though they don't usually come cheap. The traditional British Sunday lunch (roast beef and Yorkshire pudding) is a must; try one of our recommended British restaurants or any good large hotel.

Wherever you are staying you will probably get the chance to start the day the traditional British way, with a cooked breakfast of eggs, bacon and/or sausages, mushrooms, tomatoes and/or baked beans and toast. Afternoon tea is the other great English institution, comprising small thinly sliced sandwiches, scones and/or cake. At many of London's famous hotels, such as the Ritz, afternoon tea is an important daily ritual.

*Look for hand-pumped beer if you want a quality pint*

*A typical London pub along Whitehall*

61

## Did you know ?

*The raffish picture of William Shakespeare, the Chandos Portrait (painted c1610), is the sole known contemporary portrait of the Bard of Avon and is therefore claimed to be his only true likeness. It was the first picture to enter the gallery. On a similar note, there are also few original portraits of Christopher Wren in existence and the National Portrait Gallery's is one of the best.*

Below: *the world's most comprehensive portrait collection at the National Portrait Gallery*

✚ 29D3
✉ St Martin's Place, Orange Street
☎ 0171-306 0055
🕐 Mon–Sat 10–6, Sun 12–6. Closed 24–26 Dec, 1 Jan, Good Fri, May Day bank hol
🍴 Café-in-the-Crypt (£), St Martin-in-the-Fields Church
🚇 Leicester Square, Charing Cross
♿ Excellent (use Orange Street entrance)
💷 Free (except Special Exhibitions)
❓ Personal Sound Guide tour of up to 200 portraits (cheap). Frequent lectures

### NATIONAL PORTRAIT GALLERY ✪✪✪

If you've ever wanted to put a face to a famous name from British history then this is the place to do it. Founded in 1856 as the 'Gallery of the Portraits of the most eminent persons in British History', the gallery's earliest contemporary portrait is that of Henry VII, from 1505. If you want to see the exhibits in chronological order go up to the top floor and work your way down. The collection is too large to be displayed at one time so changes periodically. The pictures least likely to change are the oldest, many of which are of great historical value. Those most likely to be rotated are the portraits of late 20th-century figures; the display of new additions tends to be dictated by current public interest.

Most visitors' favourites are the very earliest (top floor), the most recent, the Victorian and the early 20th century galleries. Predictably, there are many images of royalty, and at opposite ends of the gallery is a wonderful contrast of styles featuring the likenesses of Elizabeth I and, some 400 years later, the present British queen, Elizabeth II. The Coronation Portrait of Elizabeth I is an acclaimed masterpiece, while much more controversial is the colour screenprint, in signature fashion by Andy Warhol, of the current monarch. This also underlines the point that the gallery holds more than just conventional paintings; sculptures, photography, sketches, silhouettes, caricatures and other methods of portraiture are all featured. Visitors in search of Diana, Princess of Wales, will find her on the first floor landing, alongside many members of the present royal family.

### NATURAL HISTORY MUSEUM
**(► 21, TOP TEN)**

## OXO TOWER ✪✪

Built in 1930 for the Oxo company, this splendid art deco tower has long been a Thames landmark, but in recent times had fallen into such disrepair that demolition was a likelihood. Now lovingly restored, its huge illuminated red O X O trademark letters make it one of the most striking sights on the London night skyline. The tower is now home to eating places (open daily) and award-winning craft and designer shops and studios (closed Monday). Another good reason for visiting it is to enjoy the views from the free 8th-floor public viewing gallery.

➕ 29E3
✉ Riverside Walk
☎ 0171-401 2255
🕐 Viewing gallery 11AM (sometimes earlier)–10PM
🍴 Oxo Tower restaurant (£££), brasserie (£–££)
🚇 Blackfriars, Waterloo
♿ Accessible by lift
🎟 Free

## PICCADILLY CIRCUS ✪

London's most famous circus (a site where several streets meet) is almost permanently clogged with traffic and young tourists who use the steps around the Statue of Eros as a convenient central rest stop or meeting point. It's a frenetic, unattractive place, best seen at night when the large illuminated hoardings come to life. Just off here are two youth-oriented attractions; **Rock Circus**, where Madame Tussaud's goes pop, complete with an animatronic rock show, and the tacky Trocadero, claimed to be Europe's largest indoor entertainment complex (➤ 111 and 115).

➕ 28C3
🚇 Piccadilly Circus
**Rock Circus**
✉ London Pavilion
☎ 0171-734 7203
🕐 Daily Mon, Wed, Thu, Sun 11–9, Tue 12–9, Fri–Sat 11–10
🍴 Planet Hollywood (£), Trocadero
♿ Excellent
🎟 Very expensive

*Sooner or later everyone walks through Piccadilly Circus*

✚ 28B4
🍴 Odette's (££–£££)
🚇 South of park: Regent's Park, Baker Street. North of park: Camden Town
♿ Excellent
🎫 Free

Right: *Pigeon fancier in Regent's Park*
Below: *Sir Joshua Reynold's statue still presides over the Royal Academy*

✚ 28C3
✉ Burlington House, Piccadilly
☎ 0171-300 8000. Recorded information 0171-300 5760/1
🕐 Open daily during exhibition 10–6. Closed 25 Dec
🍴 Café (£), self-service restaurant (££)
🚇 Green Park, Piccadilly Circus
♿ Excellent
🎫 Expensive
❓ Free tours of the Private Rooms, Tue–Fri 1PM

## REGENT'S PARK ✪✪✪

Like many of London's parks, this land was appropriated by Henry VIII as a royal hunting ground and was not known as Regent's Park until 1820, when the Prince Regent (the future George IV) decided to develop it as a grand new garden city. His architect was John Nash, who was also responsible for much of the magnificent building of Bath (► 88). The beautiful white sweeps of stuccoed buildings that make up the park's terraces and crescents represent only a small part of the original plans, but they remain the most elegant example of town planning in the capital.

The gardens, delightful in summer, are famous for the Zoo, Queen Mary's Rose Garden and the Regent's Park Open-air Theatre (► 112). You can also go boating on the lake.

## ROYAL ACADEMY (OF ARTS) ✪✪✪

Founded in 1768 under the presidency of the great British painter Sir Joshua Reynolds, the RA is the country's oldest fine arts society. It regularly stages world-class art exhibitions but is famous for hosting the annual Summer Exhibition (in June) which is open to both amateur and professional artists. The elegant home of the RA, Burlington House, features some fine 18th-century ceiling paintings and Britain's sole Michelangelo sculpture.

## ST BARTHOLOMEW-THE-GREAT  ✪✪

Founded in 1123 by Rahere, the court jester to Henry I, this is London's oldest church. The entrance is an unusual half-timbered Tudor gatehouse, and the atmospheric interior is reminiscent of a small cathedral. It has the best Norman chancel in London (rivalled only by the Chapel of St John in the Tower of London ➤ 24) with Norman piers supporting an upper gallery. There are also some very fine tomb monuments, including that of Rahere.

➕ 29C4
✉ Cloth Fair
☎ 0171-606 5171
🕐 Open Mon–Fri 8:30–5 (4 in winter), Sat 10:30–1:30. Sun services 8–8. Closed Mon in Aug
🍴 Fox and Anchor (£)
🚇 Barbican
♿ Access to most parts
💷 Free

---

### Did you know ?

*The landmark spire of St Bride, a 'madrigal in stone' and the tallest of any Wren church at 69m, is said to be the model for the traditional tiered wedding cake. These were first made around 200 years ago by Mr Rich, a Fleet Street pastry-cook who became famous for his spire-inspired confections.*

---

Above: *The tomb of Rahere in St Bart's. He was buried in 1143, but the monument dates from the 16th century*
Left: *Wren's masterpiece tower at St Bride*

## ST BRIDE  ✪

The Church of St Bride occupies one of the capital's oldest religious sites; during the 6th century St Bridget's Church marked the very first Irish settlement in London. The present church, completed in 1675, is a masterpiece by Christopher Wren though its interior is modern, having been gutted by a bomb in 1940. The crypt holds an interesting small museum tracing the history of the church and its long connection with the Fleet Street newspaper trade.

➕ 29E3
✉ Fleet Street
☎ 0171-353 1301
🕐 Mon–Fri 8–5, Sat 9–4:30. Sun, open for services only at 11, 6:30
🍴 Ye Olde Cheshire Cheese(£)
🚇 Blackfriars
♿ Access to church via Salisbury Court side entrance; crypt inaccessible
💷 Free
❓ Lunchtime concerts (most of year) Tue, Wed, Fri 1:15, choral services Sun 11, 6:30

➕ 28C2

✉ Chapel Royal, St James's Palace

🕐 Open for services only Sun 8:30, 11:15 (see notice board on door to confirm)

🍴 Quaglino's (£££)

🚇 Green Park

♿ Chapel Royal accessible to wheelchairs

✋ Free

❓ The St James's Palace detachment of the Queen's Guard marches to Buckingham Palace at 11:15 and returns to St James's Palace at 12:05. The Guard is changed only on days when there is a guard change at Buckingham Palace

## ST JAMES'S PALACE

After the Palace of Whitehall was destroyed in 1698, the court moved to St James's Palace, which remained the official royal London residence until 1837, when Queen Victoria decamped to Buckingham Palace. St James's still retains a royal function, however, and is the London office of the Prince of Wales. Sadly, little remains of the palace's Tudor structure except for the splendid main gatehouse in Pall Mall. The Chapel Royal (which is the only part of the palace open to the public) also retains its original exterior. Adjacent to the palace is Clarence House, home to the Queen Mother (closed to the public).

*Guardsmen at St James's Palace preparing to march off to Change the Guard at Buckingham Palace*

➕ 28C2

🚇 St James's Park

✋ Free

## ST JAMES'S PARK ✪✪

The oldest and the prettiest of central London's royal parks, St James's was established by Henry VIII in the 1530s. Charles II was the last monarch to reshape it and was often to be seen walking in the park with one of his many mistresses, or swimming in its lake. Don't miss the magical views from the bridge in the centre of the lake, west to Buckingham Palace and east to the domes and towers of Whitehall.

## ST JAMES'S PICCADILLY ★

This 'little piece of heaven in Piccadilly' was built between 1676 and 1684 by Christopher Wren, though it was badly damaged in World War II and has largely been rebuilt. The main artistic interest of the church is the work of Grinling Gibbons, the greatest woodcarver in 17th-century England. However, the church's popularity, particularly with local Londoners, lies in the numerous cultural activities it promotes, including a craft market and regular top-class concerts and recitals.

## ST JAMES'S STREET ★★

St James's is 'Gentlemen's London' and here you will find four of its most distinguished clubs: White's (No 37–8), where Prince Charles held his stag party in 1981; Boodle's (No 28), haunt of London's chief 19th-century dandy, Beau Brummell; Brooks's (No 60), renowned for its gambling; and the Carlton (No 69), bastion of the Conservative party whose male-only rules were bent for Mrs Thatcher when she was Prime Minister. Admission to all clubs is by membership only.

Of more general interest are three of London's most intriguing small shops. John Lobb's at No 9 was established in 1849 and has been 'bootmakers to the Crown' since 1911. Look inside the shop window's small museum case for historical items such as the last used for Queen Victoria's shoes. At No 6 is James Lock & Co, the 'most famous hat shop in the world', which has provided headwear for national heroes such as Nelson and Wellington and where the bowler hat was invented. The picturesque early 19th-century premises of wine merchants Berry Brothers & Rudd are at No 3, adjacent to a narrow alley leading to tiny Pickering Place where, between 1842 and 1845, the Republic of Texas kept a legation (diplomatic ministry).

---

☩ 28C3
✉ Piccadilly
☎ 0171-734 4511
🕐 Church open daily early to late depending upon activities
🍴 Wren Café (£)
Ⓠ Green Park, Piccadilly Circus
♿ Few; access via Jermyn Street
🎟 Free
❓ Concerts, recitals: Wed, Thu, Fri at 1:10 (free). Evening concerts most Thu, Fri, Sat at 7:30 (very expensive). Craft market Thu–Sat 10–6

*Above & left: Lock & Co, where the Duke of Wellington bought the plumed hat that he wore at the Battle of Waterloo*

☩ 28C2
Ⓠ Green Park

## ST KATHARINE'S DOCK ⚫⚫

➕ 85D3
🍴 Dickens Inn (£)
🚇 Tower Hill
🎫 Free

To experience the flavour of London's huge dockland warehouses as they used to be without making the journey east, visit St Katharine's Dock, conveniently close to the Tower of London. Here exotic items such as ostrich feathers, spices, teas, turtles and ivory (up to 22,000 tusks in a year) were once stored. The Dock was closed in 1968 and subsequently developed to cater for the tourist trade with shops, restaurants and historic sailing ships at berth. The picturesque Dickens Inn pub-restaurant incorporates 17th-century timbers into its galleried frontage.

## ST PAUL'S CATHEDRAL (➤ 22, TOP TEN)

## ST STEPHEN WALBROOK ⚫⚫

➕ 29F3
✉ 39 Walbrook
☎ 0171-283 4444
🕐 Mon–Thu 10–4, Fri 10–3
🍴 Sweetings (££) (➤ 96)
🚇 Bank, Cannon Street
♿ Few
🎫 Free

This is the Lord Mayor of London's parish church and is arguably the finest of all the City's churches. Built by Christopher Wren between 1672 and 1679, its dome was the first in England and was clearly a prototype for Wren's engineering *tour de force*, the dome of St Paul's Cathedral. The church was beautifully restored between 1978 and 1987, with the original dark-wood fittings making a striking contrast to the gleaming white marble floor and the controversial giant white 'Camembert cheese' stone altarpiece, designed by Sir Henry Moore in 1972.

Above: *unable to take large ships, St Katharine's Dock was never a commercial success*
Right: *trial run for St Paul's: St Stephen Walbrook*

## SCIENCE MUSEUM (➤ 23, TOP TEN)

## SHAKESPEARE'S GLOBE EXHIBITION ★★

In May 1997 the dream of American film and theatre director, the late Sam Wanamaker, was finally realised when his faithful reconstruction of Shakespeare's circular wooden Globe Theatre was completed after 25 years. Built strictly according to contemporary late 16th-century techniques, it is the first thatched building that has been erected in London since the Great Fire of 1666. The Globe Exhibition tells the story behind this remarkable project and the entrance fee includes a look inside the theatre.

✚ 29E3
✉ New Globe Walk, Bankside
☎ 0171-902 1500
🕐 May–mid-Sep Mon 9:15–4:45, Tue–Sat 9:15–12:15, Sun 9:15–2:15. Mid-Sep–May daily 10–5. Closed 24, 25 Dec
🍴 Globe Café (£), Globe Restaurant (££)
Ⓜ Mansion House
♿ Very good
💷 Moderate
❓ Tours every half hour

Above: *Shakespeare's Globe Theatre*
Left: *Sir John Soane's collection, untouched since the mid 18th-century.*

## SIR JOHN SOANE'S MUSEUM ★★★

In terms of size and layout, this extraordinary labyrinthine museum, which occupies three adjoining medium-sized houses, is the most unusual art and antiquities collection in the capital. It was formerly the home of the designer and architect Sir John Soane (1753–1837) and has, according to the terms specified by Soane himself, been kept exactly in its original condition. Much of this magpie collection is arranged around a central court and is aided and abetted by false walls, alcoves, domes and skylights. Its treasures include pictures by Turner, Canaletto and Hogarth (including the famous *Rake's Progress* series), a sarcophagus from the Valley of the Kings, a bizarre Gothic folly entitled the 'Monk's Parlour', plus sculptures and stone fragments galore. See it and believe it!

✚ 29D3
✉ 13 Lincoln's Inn Fields
☎ 0171-430 0175
🕐 Tue–Sat 10–5. Closed all public hols
🍴 October Gallery Café (£)
Ⓜ Holborn
♿ Most of ground floor accessible
💷 Free (charge for exhibitions)
❓ Excellent guided tour Sat 2:30 (cheap)

➕ 28C3
🍴 Many options available
Ⓜ Piccadilly Circus,
   Tottenham Court Rd,
   Oxford Circus

*Soho's Chinatown is one
of the best places for
cheap and interesting
food in the capital*

➕ 29F3
✉ Cathedral Street
☎ 0171-407 3708
🕐 Daily 8–6
🍴 Pizza Express (£) in
   cathedral chapter house
Ⓜ London Bridge
♿ Good
🎟 Free

➕ 28C2
✉ 27 St James's Place
☎ 0171-499 8620
🕐 Sun 10:30–4:45. Closed
   Jan, Aug
Ⓜ Green Park
♿ Very good
🎟 Expensive
❓ No children under ten

### SOHO

Soho, bounded roughly by Oxford Street, Regent Street, Coventry Street/Leicester Square and Charing Cross Road, is central London's most cosmopolitan area. Over the centuries it has accommodated waves of French Huguenot, Italian, Greek and latterly Chinese immigrants, and artists too have long been drawn here, giving Soho its Bohemian reputation. In the 1960s and 1970s the area became notorious for sleaze, though a clean-up in the 1980s closed some of the worst establishments. Today the area is known for its many reasonably priced restaurants, its buzzing nightlife, and more recently, as a gay centre.

### SOUTHWARK CATHEDRAL

Often overlooked by visitors, Southwark Cathedral boasts one of the oldest and most interesting church interiors in the capital. Construction began in 1220 and was finished some 200 years later (though most of its exterior features were remodelled much later). The nave retains some original stonework and fascinating 15th-century bosses – one depicts the devil swallowing Judas Iscariot. There are several grand monuments, the most notable being to the area's most famous parishioner, William Shakespeare, who lived in Southwark from 1599 to 1611. His brother Edmund (died 1607) and other fellow dramatists are buried in the cathedral.

### SPENCER HOUSE

Built between 1756 and 1766 for Earl Spencer (an ancestor of the late Diana, Princess of Wales), Spencer House is London's finest surviving mid-18th-century house. Indeed, it has been described as London's most magnificent private palace. After being completely restored at a cost of £16 million, it was opened to visitors in 1990. The 1-hour guided tour takes in eight rooms featuring elegant gilded decorations and period paintings and furniture.

## TATE GALLERY ✪✪✪

The Tate, one of Britain's foremost galleries, is home to two national collections; British art from the 16th century onwards, and international modern art. The former is often forgotten, lost in the furore of publicity that generally accompanies new and frequently controversial exhibitions of the latter, which culminates in a media frenzy each November when the prestigious annual Turner Prize for Modern Art is awarded.

It is impossible to say what will be on display at any one time as the Tate has insufficient space to show all its works at once. Displays change each year, with 'surplus' exhibits either going into storage, or to branch museums at Liverpool and St Ives. Moreover, the Tate is in the throes of transferring its international collection just across the Thames to the former Bankside Power Station. This is due to open its doors as the Tate Gallery of Modern Art in 2000, leaving just the British art collection in the present Millbank gallery site.

The highlight of the British collection is the Turner Bequest, comprising many of the finest works of J M W Turner, regarded by many as Britain's greatest landscape painter. The Tate also has a superb collection of High Victorian and Pre-Raphaelite pictures.

✚ 29D1
✉ Millbank
☎ 0171-887 8000 Recorded information 0171-887 8008
🕐 Daily 10–5:50
🍽 Tate Café (£); Tate Restaurant (£££) ☎ 0171-887 8825
Ⓜ Westminster
♿ Excellent
🎟 Free (charge for exhibitions)
❓ Free guided tours Mon–Sat 11, 12, 2, 3. TateInform personal audio guide (cheap). Art Trolley activities for children (aged 4+) Sun 2–5

Left: *The Tate Gallery was founded in 1897 by the sugar tycoon Sir Henry Tate*

## THEATRE MUSEUM ✪

For the casual visitor, the best thing about this National Museum of the Performing Arts is its free-of-charge foyer, set in theatrical darkness with a re-creation of a gilded Edwardian theatre box and numerous spectacular contemporary and historical costumes. The bulk of the collection is devoted to the history of the British theatre and is unlikely to make converts. If you have a predilection for greasepaint and the boards, however, make the most of the collection by taking a guided tour and joining in the costume workshop and make-up demonstrations.

✚ 29D3
✉ Russell Street
☎ 0171-836 7891
🕐 Tue–Sun 11–7
🍽 Chez Gérard at the Opera Terrace (££)
Ⓜ Covent Garden
♿ Excellent
🎟 Cheap

London Travel Information 0171-222 1234 24 hours
Minicom 0171-918 3015

© London Regional Transport

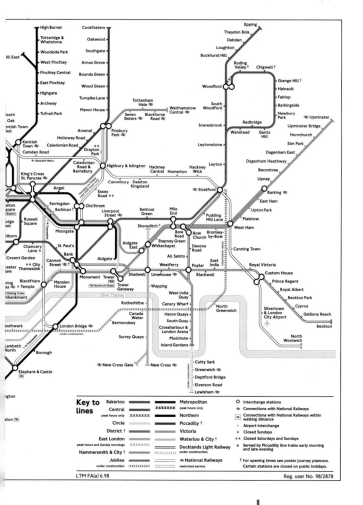

**Key to lines**

Bakerloo
Central — peak hours only
Circle
District †
East London — peak hours and Sunday mornings
Hammersmith & City †
Jubilee — under construction

Metropolitan
— peak hours only
Northern
Piccadilly †
Victoria
Waterloo & City † —
Docklands Light Railway — under construction
National Railways
— restricted service

○ Interchange stations
⇌ Connections with National Railways
▢ Connections with National Railways within walking distance
✈ Airport interchange
✦ Closed Sundays
✦✦ Closed Saturdays and Sundays
A Served by Piccadilly line trains early morning and late evening

† For opening times see poster journey planners.
Certain stations are closed on public holidays.

LTM FA(a) 6.98

Reg. user No. 98/2878

- 29F2
- Tower Bridge
- 0171-403 3761 (Tower Bridge Experience)
- Apr–Oct 10–6:30, Nov–Mar 9:30–6. Last admission 75 min before closing
- Butler's Wharf Chop House (£££)
- Tower Hill
- Most areas accessible by lift
- Expensive
- Occasional twilight tours offering magnificent views of London

### TOWER BRIDGE ✪✪✪

One of London's best-known landmarks, Tower Bridge was built between 1886 and 1894 and hailed as one of the greatest engineering feats of its day. It is basically a classic Victorian iron and steel structure, clad in stone to match the medieval appearance of its neighbour, the Tower of London. Until quite recently it was the last road bridge across the Thames before the river reaches the North Sea, and remains London's only drawbridge. This function was to allow large ships to pass into the busy Upper Pool of London, which was a hive of warehouse activity in Victorian times. At its peak, its bascules were like yo-yos, up and down 50 times a day. Today they open on average just four to five times a week.

The structure now houses the Tower Bridge Experience, an informative and highly entertaining multi-media exhibition which explains the history of the bridge through the use of animatronic characters, holograms and interactive computers. You can also step right into the bowels of the building to see the original Victorian engine rooms. The high-level walkways, 43m above the river, were designed to allow pedestrians to cross when the drawbridges were raised, and the views are unbeatable. Even from ground level, however, Tower Bridge is one of the capital's great vantage points.

**TOWER OF LONDON (► 24, TOP TEN)**

### Did you know ?

*Tower Bridge contains over 27,000 tons of bricks, enough to build around 350 detached houses. An average of 432 men worked for nearly 2,900 days on it, and the final cost was around £1.2 million. The bridge is 268m long from shore to shore and its drawbridges each weigh 1,000 tons.*

## TRAFALGAR SQUARE ✪✪✪

This is the geographical and symbolic centre of London; all road distances are measured from here and, at its centre, Nelson's Column is one of London's most potent symbols. The grandiose buildings of South Africa House, Canada House and the National Gallery line three sides of the square, while the fourth opens to Whitehall. The square takes its name from the Battle of Trafalgar in 1805, during which Admiral Nelson, Britain's greatest naval hero, commanded his fleet to the famous victory against Franco-Spanish forces. Nelson was killed during the battle and the 57m-high column was erected between 1839 and 1842.

The church on the square, with its landmark tower dramatically floodlit by night, is **St Martin-in-the-Fields**, built in 1726 by James Gibbs. This handsome building is famous for concerts and is also a thriving community centre with a social care unit and several minor visitor attractions. Above ground it hosts a daily clothes and crafts market, while its famous crypt houses an art gallery, the London Brass Rubbing Centre, gift shops and the excellent Café-in-the-Crypt.

## VICTORIA AND ALBERT MUSEUM (▶ 25, TOP TEN)

✚ 29D3

**St Martin-in-the-Fields**

✉ Trafalgar Square

☎ General enquiries 0171-930 0089; concert enquiries 0171-839 8362

🕐 Church open 8AM. Crypt open Mon–Sat 10–8, Sun 12–8. Lunchtime concerts Mon, Tue, Fri at 1:05. Candlelit concerts of baroque music most Thu–Sat eves

🍽 Café-in-the-Crypt (£)

🚇 Charing Cross, Leicester Square

♿ Ramp access to church, no wheelchair access to café

🎫 Free. Lunchtime concerts free, charge for evening concerts

+ 28B3

✉ Hertford House,
  Manchester Square

☎ 0171-935 0687

🕐 Mon–Sat 10–5, Sun 2–5

🍴 Stephen Bull, W1 (£££)

Ⓜ Bond Street

♿ All areas accessible; no
  electric wheelchairs

✋ Free

❓ General guided tours
  (free) Mon–Fri 1 (Wed
  also 11:30), Sat 11:30,
  Sun 3

### WALLACE COLLECTION ✪✪✪

This is one of the capital's hidden gems, the perfect antidote to the bustle of nearby Oxford Street. The collection is housed in the peaceful surroundings of a small stately home and you can enjoy some of London's finest works of art while clocks tick gently, secure in the knowledge that there will be only a handful of fellow visitors to disturb your concentration.

The predominant theme of the collection, the legacy of the inveterate 19th-century collector, Sir Richard Wallace, is French 18th-century art. Downstairs, the André Boulle furniture (including pieces made for the Palace of Versailles), is truly staggering, both in opulence and sheer bulk. Alongside is the best museum collection of Sèvres porcelain in the world. Less well known is the Wallace's magnificent collection of arms and armour – arguably the equal of that in the Tower of London. Upstairs in the picture galleries the Gallic theme continues. The most notable exception is the famous Gallery 22, where, among works by Rubens, Rembrandt, Claude and Velázquez, the star exhibits are the *Laughing Cavalier* by Frans Hals and *Perseus and Andromeda* by Titian.

### WESTMINSTER ABBEY (▶ 26, TOP TEN)

### WESTMINSTER CATHEDRAL ✪

+ 28C2

✉ Victoria Street

☎ 0171-798 9055

🕐 Mon–Fri 7AM–8PM (closes
  7PM in winter), Sat–Sun
  7AM–8:30PM (opens 8AM
  in winter). Campanile lift
  mid-Mar–Oct daily 9–5

Ⓜ Victoria

♿ Accessible to
  wheelchairs

✋ Cathedral free; campanile
  cheap

Not to be confused with the more illustrious abbey of the same name, Westminster Cathedral is London's principal Roman Catholic church. Its foundation is relatively modern, being built between 1896 and 1903. The slim, handsome Byzantine campanile is one of the capital's lesser-known landmarks, towering some 83m high and offering great views over central London. The cathedral interior is famous for some of the finest and most varied marble-work in the country, though it has never been completed (owing to lack of funds) and much of the huge nave ceiling still shows bare brickwork.

*Westminster cathedral is a brick masterpiece with 12.5 million in all and no steel reinforcements*

*True Brit: 10 Downing Street (above) and Guardsman at Horse Guards (left)*

## WHITEHALL ★★

Whitehall has been the country's principal corridor of power since the early 18th century. The epicentre is Downing Street, home to the Prime Minister and to the Chancellor of the Exchequer, while to north and south are various grey and sober buildings which house the country's top civil servants and ministries. Just south of Downing Street is the Cenotaph, the national memorial to the dead of the two World Wars. The street was named after Henry VIII's Whitehall Palace, which burned down in 1698, leaving the Banqueting House (➤ 33) as the sole surviving building above ground. Opposite here is Horse Guards, the historic, official entrance to the royal palaces, still guarded by two mounted troopers and a good place to watch one of London's least fussy, least crowded guard-changing ceremonies.

✚ 29D2
⏲ No public access to Downing Street
🍴 Café-in-the-Crypt (£)
🚇 South end Westminster ; north end Charing Cross
❓ Horse Guards guard changes 11AM Mon–Sat, 10AM Sun; ceremonial dismounting and inspection daily at 4. National Remembrance Service held at the Cenotaph at 11AM on Sun nearest 11 Nov

## WINSTON CHURCHILL'S BRITAIN AT WAR ★★

Sheltered appropriately deep beneath the arches of London Bridge, this is an evocative museum of what it was like to live in the capital during the dark and dangerous period of World War II, and particularly during the Blitz of 1940–1. Aside from examining a huge number of well-displayed original period objects, you can sit in an air-raid shelter or walk through an eerily authentic bombed-out building. Older visitors will enjoy the bitter-sweet nostalgia of such displays as life on the Home Front, evacuation, movie news and re-created shopfronts, while younger ones will enjoy the drama but no doubt be grateful they didn't experience the traumas of those years.

✚ 29F2
✉ 64–6 Tooley Street
☎ 0171-403 3171
⏲ Daily 10–5:30 (Oct–Mar 4:30)
🍴 Café dell 'Ugo (£–££), Tooley Street
🚇 London Bridge
♿ Excellent
💷 Expensive

# Outer London &
# Beyond

When the crowds and noise of central London begin to make you wonder if you made the right choice by taking a city holiday, it's time to head out of town: fortunately you don't have to go far before the whole atmosphere changes.

The easiest and most popular excursion is downriver to Greenwich, full of history, good shopping and restaurants. Upriver lie Hampton Court and Kew Gardens. Each makes a glorious sunny summer's day out, but don't try to combine the two – there is far too much to see. Return visitors to London should seek out the low-key but highly enjoyable pleasures of riverside Richmond and Twickenham.

If you have time to leave the metropolis for a day or two, Bath is an urban dream; Oxford and Cambridge are fascinating for their universities; while Windsor Castle is a treat for lovers of history and royalty.

> '*Thy Forests, Windsor!*
> *and thy green Retreats.*
> *At once the Monarch's and*
> *the Muse's Seats*'

ALEXANDER POPE,
*Windsor-Forest*, 1713

———————•———————

Left: *Cutty Sark*

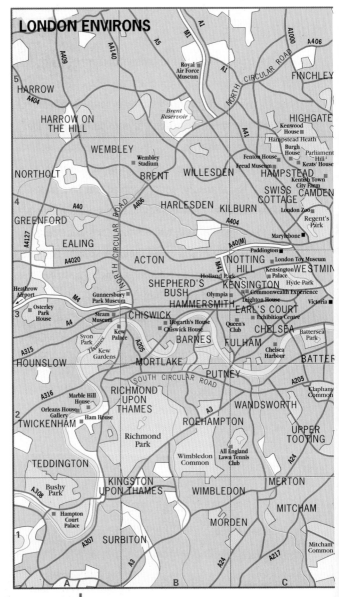

# LONDON ENVIRONS

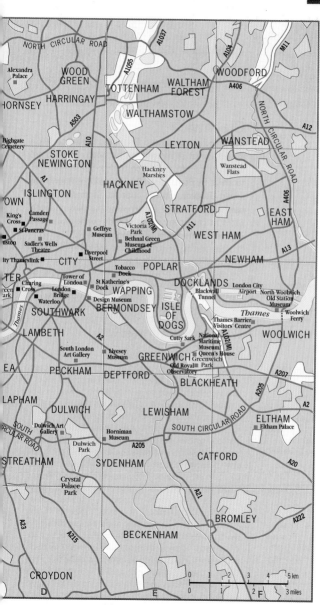

NORTH CIRCULAR ROAD
A1037
A104
M11

Alexandra Palace
WOOD GREEN
A1055
TOTTENHAM
WALTHAM FOREST
WOODFORD
A406

HORNSEY
HARRINGAY
A503
WALTHAMSTOW
NORTH CIRCULAR ROAD
A12

Highgate Cemetery
A10
LEYTON
WANSTEAD
A406

STOKE NEWINGTON
Hackney Marshes
Wanstead Flats

A1
ISLINGTON
HACKNEY
A102(M)
STRATFORD
A11
EAST HAM

'OWN
King's Cross
Camden Passage
Geffrye Museum
Victoria Park
Bethnal Green Museum of Childhood
WEST HAM
A13

uston
St Pancras
Sadler's Wells Theatre
Liverpool Street
NEWHAM

ity Thameslink
CITY
Tobacco Dock
POPLAR
DOCKLANDS
London City Airport
North Woolwich Old Station Museum

TER
'cen
ark
Charing Cross
Tower of London
London Bridge
Waterloo
St Katherine's Dock
Design Museum
WAPPING
BERMONDSEY
Blackwall Tunnel
ISLE OF DOGS
Thames
Woolwich Ferry

Thames
SOUTHWARK
LAMBETH
A2
Thames Barrier Visitors' Centre
A102(M)
WOOLWICH

EA
South London Art Gallery
Livesey Museum
Cutty Sark
National Maritime Museum
Queen's House
Greenwich Park

PECKHAM
DEPTFORD
GREENWICH
Old Royal Observatory
BLACKHEATH
A207

LAPHAM
DULWICH
LEWISHAM
SOUTH CIRCULAR ROAD
ELTHAM
A2

SOUTH IRCULAR ROAD
Dulwich Art Gallery
Horniman Museum
Eltham Palace

Dulwich Park
A205
CATFORD
A20

STREATHAM
SYDENHAM

A23
A215
Crystal Palace Park
A21

BROMLEY
A222

BECKENHAM

CROYDON
D
E
F

0  1  2  3  4  5 km
0  1  2  3 miles

*The Royal Naval College,
designed by
Sir Christopher Wren
as a hospital for naval
pensioners*

# Greenwich

**Greenwich (pronounced Gren-itch) lies some 10km (6 miles) east of the centre of London. You can get there by train from London Bridge, but it's far nicer to arrive by boat, or by Docklands Light Railway to Island Gardens, directly opposite Greenwich. From here you can enjoy a river view that has changed little in centuries, then simply walk under the Thames via the Greenwich Foot Tunnel.**

Though suffering from heavy traffic and summer crowds, Greenwich retains something of a village atmosphere with lots of interesting small shops, a throbbing market, an abundance of historic attractions and one of London's finest parks. Greenwich is also the site of the Millennium Dome, the focal point of Britain's millennium celebrations.

## What to See in Greenwich

### NATIONAL MARITIME MUSEUM ✪✪✪

The old and rather tired-looking National Maritime Museum is in the process of being rebuilt and expanded. By the time work is complete (all galleries due to be reopened by summer 1999) it will reconfirm its status as the world's largest and most important maritime museum.

The new centre of the museum is the Neptune Court, a dramatic glassed-over courtyard holding the museum's largest objects, such as the magnificent carved and gilded state barge made for Frederick, Prince of Wales, in 1732. Off here are 15 or so major galleries that explain the history and role of maritime Greenwich, Britain as a once-great sea power and more worldwide topics such as international cargo shipping and ocean exploration. Some of the finest ship models ever made and great maritime paintings are also here. Younger visitors should head for Waterworld, which explains the marine environment, and to All Hands, a great hands-on place for budding seafarers. Britain's greatest naval hero, Admiral Lord Nelson, gets pride of place in his own gallery covering his fascinating career and private life in tremendous detail.

## OLD ROYAL OBSERVATORY ✪✪

The Royal Observatory was founded in 1675 by Charles II to find out the 'so-much desired longitude of places for perfecting the art of (sea) navigation'. Set high on a mound in Greenwich Park, and commanding a splendid view (even today), it was designed by Christopher Wren and functioned as Britain's principal observatory until 1945. Today it is a museum that tells the history of the observatory and offers a crash course in the measurement of time and astronomy. This is not an easy subject to grasp, but displays are well explained and feature some beautiful historical instruments. There is also a fascinating camera obscura to visit. The prime attraction for most visitors, however, is to be photographed standing astride the 0° longitude line (which passes right through the observatory) with one foot in the eastern hemisphere and one foot in the western hemisphere.

The distinctive dome of the Old Royal Observatory

- ✚ 85E3
- ✉ Greenwich Park
- ☎ Recorded information 0181-312 6565
- 🕐 Daily 10–5 (last admission 4:30). Closed 24–26 Dec
- 🍴 Bosun's Café (£), National Maritime Museum
- 🚢 River boat to Greenwich Pier
- Ⓖ DLR to Island Gardens, then foot tunnel.
- 🚉 Greenwich from London Bridge
- ♿ Not all the buildings are fully accessible. Special access days can be arranged ☎ 0181-858 4422
- 💷 Moderate/expensive. Combined ticket also gives access to National Maritime Museum and Queen's House and is valid for one return visit within 12 months

## QUEEN'S HOUSE ✪✪

This exquisite miniature palace is set at the heart of Greenwich's historic riverfront complex and was the very first classical-style building in England, begun in 1616. It was designed by Inigo Jones. The queen in question was originally Anne of Denmark, wife of James I, though by the time of completion in 1635 she had died and Henrietta Maria, wife of Charles I, assumed tenancy.

- ✚ 85E3
- ✉ Greenwich Park
- ☎ Recorded information 0181-312 6565
- 🕐 Daily 10–5 (last admission 4:30). Closed 24–26 Dec
- 🍴 Bosun's Café (£), National Maritime Museum
- 🚢 River boat to Greenwich Pier
- Ⓖ DLR to Island Gardens, then foot tunnel.
- 🚉 Greenwich from London Bridge
- ♿ Partial access. Special access days can be arranged ☎ 0181-858 4422
- 💷 Moderate/expensive.

### Did you know ?

*Contrary to popular legend, Admiral Lord Nelson never wore an eye patch, though he did have a special hat (on display in Westminster Abbey's Undercroft Museum) to shade the eye that he injured at the Battle of Calvi. The bullet-holed jacket and blood-stained clothing that Nelson wore at the Battle of Trafalgar is in the museum's Nelson Gallery.*

# Around Greenwich

**Distance**
Approximately 3km (1¾ miles)

**Time**
2–4 hours, depending on visits

**Start point**
✚ 40A1
Greenwich Pier
🚤 River boat to Greenwich
Pier
Ⓔ DLR to Island Gardens,
then foot tunnel.
🚉 Greenwich from London
Bridge

**End point**
✚ 40A1
Royal Naval College (next to
Greenwich Pier)

**Lunch**
Goddard's Ye Old Pie House
(➤ 52), or picnic in the park
✉ 45 Greenwich Church
Street

**Cutty Sark**
☎ 0181-858 2698
🕐 Mon–Sat 10–5/6, Sun
12–5/6,
👣 Moderate

**Royal Naval College and
Chapel**
☎ 0181-858 2154
🕐 Daily 2:30–4:45
👣 Free

*The view from the
Observatory across to
Docklands*

The maritime heritage of Greenwich is immediately apparent even before you land at Greenwich Pier, where tall masts and rigging signpost the *Cutty Sark*. Launched in 1869, this is the last surviving British sailing clipper and is famous for its colourful collection of ships' figureheads. Close by is *Gipsy Moth IV*, the tiny craft in which Sir Francis Chichester became the first Englishman to single-handedly sail around the world in 1966–7 (closed to the public).

> *Walk up Greenwich Church Street (pick up a map at the tourist information office) and go through the market (➤ 109) to emerge on King William Walk. Turn right and enter Greenwich Park.*

Follow any of the paths that lead up to the Old Royal Observatory (➤ 83) from where you can enjoy one of London's finest views.

> *Continue along Blackheath Avenue.*

Turn left towards the bandstand, the lovely park gardens and the adjacent wilderness area where deer have been resident for centuries.

> *Walk back downhill and exit the park near the boating pond into Park Row, then turn left into Romney Road to the entrance to the Royal Naval Chapel.*

This majestic baroque complex was built by Christopher Wren between 1694 and 1745 as a home for Royal Naval Pensioners. They left here in 1869 and until recently the building was used as a Royal Naval College.

# What to See around Outer London

### HAMPTON COURT PALACE ★★★

Work on Hampton Court Palace began in 1514 under the tenure of Henry VIII's Lord Chancellor, Cardinal Wolsey. By 1528, however, Wolsey had fallen from favour and Henry had acquired it for himself. He built it up to be the most lavish palace in England where he fêted European royalty and spent five of his six honeymoons. William III and Mary II commissioned Christopher Wren to remodel the apartments and to give the palace much of its present-day appearance. George II was the last monarch to use Hampton Court.

For most visitors the Tudor survivals are still the palace highlights; the great gatehouse and a magnificent astronomical clock, the capacious Tudor Kitchens stocked with contemporary foods and utensils, and fires ablaze all year round, the sumptuous centrepiece Great Hall and the Chapel Royal with its breathtaking ceiling. The King's Apartments (built by William III) are among the finest baroque state apartments in the world and the Wolsey Rooms hold a fine Renaissance picture gallery, though the palace's greatest artwork, *Triumphs of Caesar* by Mantegna, is in the orangery. The gardens, planted in the late 17th century, are glorious and include the ever-popular maze, the Great Vine (England's largest) and the Royal Tennis Court. The latter was built in 1626 and real tennis (a hybrid of squash and lawn tennis) is still played here regularly.

☩ 28A1
✉ Hampton Court
☎ 0181-781 9500
🕐 Daily: mid Mar–mid Oct Tue–Sun 9:30–6, Mon 10:15–6. Mid Oct–mid Mar closes 4:30
🍴 Garden café (£) and restaurant (£££)
🚉 Train from Waterloo direct to Hampton Court. Boat from Westminster, Richmond or Kingston
🚌 111, 216, 461, 513, R68. Green Line Coach from Victoria 415, 718
♿ Excellent
🎟 All-inclusive ticket to palace and gardens very expensive. Gardens free. Privy garden: summer cheap; winter free.

*Above: Hampton Court Palace is famous for its gardens and holds a flower show every July*

✚ 84A3

☎ 0181-940 1171

🕐 Daily from 9:30. Closes
3:30 winter, summer
7:30 ☎ 0181-940 1171
Closed 25 Dec, 1 Jan

🍴 Café (£), restaurant (£–££)

🚇 Kew Gardens. Riverboat
to Kew pier from
Westminster and
Richmond (summer only)

♿ All areas except Marianne
North gallery accessible

💷 Moderate

❓ Tours (cheap) daily:
winter 11, rest of
year 11, 2

*Above: Kew Gardens's
greenhouses replicate
even the driest of climates*

*Right: the Pagoda built in
1761 towers 50m high;
sadly it is not open to the
public*

*Opposite: Ham House
features one of the finest
Stuart interiors in the
country and lovely gardens*

## KEW GARDENS
## (ROYAL BOTANIC GARDENS)   ✪✪✪

Founded in the late 18th century, Kew Gardens, a huge park of almost 122ha, holds a marvellous collection of plants, trees and flowers from every corner of the globe. Most of the species are grown outdoors, but huge glass and wrought iron greenhouses replicate exotic climes – from rainforest, to swamp, to desert. The most spectacular of these is the curvy Palm House, built between 1844 and 1848. The Temperate House was the world's largest greenhouse when built in 1899 and contains a Chilean Wine Palm some 18m tall and over 150 years old. The Princess of Wales Conservatory is a favourite for its giant water-lily pads, and the new Evolution House is a high-tech exploration of the story of the planet to date.

Reminders of the gardens' early royal patronage are provided by tiny Kew Palace (closed until 2001), Queen Charlotte's Cottage and the secluded Queen's Garden. Also within the gardens are some notable follies, including Kew's distinctive ten-storey pagoda, plus museums and art galleries.

## RICHMOND AND TWICKENHAM ✪✪✪

These adjoining riverside suburbs just west of town make up one of London's most charming and bucolic districts. From Richmond station turn left to walk along George Street. Off here to the right is a lovely village green. Return to George Street and continue to Richmond Bridge and the impressive new classical-style riverside development. To visit Richmond Park take bus 371 and get off at the Royal Star & Garter; here you can enjoy the magnificent view down on to the river that has been painted by numerous artists, including J M W Turner.

Richmond Park, London's largest royal park and one of its wildest, with herds of deer, makes an ideal place for a picnic. If you want to explore it properly consider hiring a bicycle. As an alternative to the park, follow the towpath along the river from Richmond Bridge (it's possible to cycle along here) and after around 30 minutes you will reach Ham House. This is an outstanding 17th-century house which has been refurbished to its former glory.

To get to Twickenham (on the opposite side of the river) walk back a short way to the Hammerston Ferry and cross to Marble Hill House, a lovely Palladian villa built for a mistress of George II in the early 1720s. A short walk further on is Orleans House Gallery where temporary art exhibitions are staged in a beautiful baroque octagon room. To return to Richmond, walk up Orleans Road and catch any one of several buses that run along the Richmond Road.

**Tourist Information Office**
- 84A2
- Old Town Hall, Richmond
- ☎ 0181-940 9125
- Mon–Fri 10–6, Sat 10–5, Sun (May–Oct only) 10:15–4:15

**Ham House**
- Ham Street, Ham
- ☎ 0181-940 1950
- House Mar–Oct Sat–Wed 1–5. Gdns all year
- Moderate

**Marble Hill House**
- Richmond Road, Twickenham
- ☎ 0181-892 5115
- Daily Apr–Sep 10–6 Nov–Mar Wed–Sun 10–4
- Cheap

**Orleans House Gallery**
- Riverside, Twickenham
- ☎ 0181-892 0221
- Tue–Sat 11–5, Sun 1–4; (May–Oct only)
- Free

# Excursions away from London

## BATH

Recently designated as a UNESCO world heritage site, the honey-coloured city of Bath was developed as a fashionable spa in the 18th century and is a perfect example of a Georgian town. It was the **Roman Baths** that first established the city and, still remarkably complete, they form the most impressive Roman remains in Britain. Adjacent is another 'must-see' site, Bath Abbey, dating mostly from the 16th century. A short walk away is the **Royal Crescent**, built between 1767 and 1774. This glorious terrace of 30 classically inspired three-storey houses in glowing golden Bath stone is often claimed to be the most majestic street in Britain.

Just outside Bath, at Claverton, is the excellent **American Museum**, which features 18 authentically re-created 17th- to 19th-century rooms.

*Right: Elegant Georgian façades: The Circus, Bath*

## CAMBRIDGE

Cambridge is famous for its university, one of the oldest and most prestigious in Britain, alongside Oxford. The oldest college is Peterhouse, founded in1284, but the most noted college is King's, established in 1441 and renowned for its magnificent medieval architecture and almost heavenly choir. Outstanding among the other 31 colleges are Queen's, Trinity, Magdalene, St John's, Clare, Jesus and Emmanuel. All the colleges now admit both men and women, but Magdalene has only done this since 1988.

The Backs is a strip of grassy meadow-cum-lawns between the rear of the colleges and the River Cam. It is a fine venue for a picnic and is a good place for college viewing. Spanning the Cam are two famous bridges: the Bridge of Sighs, a copy of the famous Venetian bridge; and the Mathematical Bridge, a wooden crossing now bolted together but originally assembled without a single metal fixing. The town's principal museum is the **Fitzwilliam Museum**, with outstanding collections of paintings, antiquities, ceramics and armour.

# Around Oxford

Start from the tourist information centre, where you can pick up maps and leaflets.

*Turn right into St Aldate's Street and enter Christ Church college through the War Memorial Garden. Exit left from the gate by the Picture Gallery into Oriel Square, named after the college on the right-hand side. Visit the college grounds then continue up Oriel Street to High Street, where you emerge opposite the splendid 17th-century portico of the University Church of St Mary the Virgin. Visit the church, then leave from the rear entrance into Radcliffe Square.*

On your left is Brasenose College, while in the centre of the square is the Radcliffe Camera, built in 1749 and now part of the **Bodleian Library**. There is no entry for the public to this building but the magnificent rooms of the main library (in neighbouring Schools Quad) are open.

*Go through Schools Quad and turn left at the far end*

The domed **Sheldonian Theatre** ahead was designed by Christopher Wren between 1663 and 1669. Climb to the top for a view of Oxford's 'dreaming spires'.

*Leave the Sheldonian and walk straight ahead, crossing Catte Street, and beneath Oxford's very own Bridge of Sighs across Queen's Lane.*

For a pub lunch turn immediately left into St Helen's Passage and follow it to the famous Turf Tavern.

*Return to New College Lane and follow this around to New College, noting the splendid gargoyles and grotesques on the wall. Leaving New College, Queen's Lane takes you between Queen's College (right) and St Edmund Hall (also a college, left).*

Turn right on to the High Street and walk a little further to Magdalen College (pronounced 'Mordlin'), with luck in time to attend the famous Evensong performance (generally at 6PM, but check with the tourist information centre).

**Distance**
Approx 5km (3 miles)

**Time**
4–6 hours depending on which colleges are open

**Start point**
Tourist information centre

**End point**
Magdalen College

**Lunch**
Turf Tavern (£)
✉ Bath Place, via St Helen's Passage

**Bodleian Library**
✉ Broad Street
☎ 01865-277165
🕐 Guided tours Mon–Fri 10:30, 11:30, 2, 3. Sat 10:30, 11:30
💷 Moderate
♿ Wheelchair access ground floor only; phone in advance

**Sheldonian Theatre**
✉ Broad Street
🕐 Mon–Sat 10–12:30, 2–3:30 (subject to functions)
💷 Cheap

**Tourist Information Centre**
- ✉ The Old School,
  Gloucester Green
- ☎ 01865-726871

**Ashmolean Museum**
- ✉ Beaumont Street
- ☎ 01865-278000
- 🕐 Tue–Sat 10–4, Sun 2–4.
  Closed Mon
- ✋ Free

**Tourist Information Centre**
- ✉ 24 High Street
- ☎ 01753-743900
- 🕐 Mon–Fri 10–4, Sat–Sun
  10–5. Extended hours in
  summer

**Windsor Castle**
- ✉ Entrance on Castle Hill
- ☎ 01753-868286 ext 2615.
  24-hour recorded
  information 01753-
  831118
- 🕐 Daily: Mar–Oct 10–5:30
  (last admission 4);
  Nov–Feb 10–4 (last
  admission 3). St George's
  Chapel only open for
  services on Sun
- ✋ Very expensive

## OXFORD ✪✪✪

Oxford is synonymous with its university, the oldest in Britain. The most outstanding colleges are Christ Church, New College and Magdalen. Oxford also has plenty of non-university attractions, including the **Ashmolean Museum**, home to one of Britain's finest provincial collections, and the Pitt-Rivers Museum, an extraordinary and delightfully old-fashioned Victorian ethnographic treasure-trove. The charming Covered Market selling food and clothing, plus all sorts of other things, is also worth a visit.

## WINDSOR ✪✪✪

Windsor is famous above all for its spectacularly sited **castle**, which (like the Tower of London) dates back to the time of William the Conqueror and has been continuously occupied since the 11th century. It has been enlarged and remodelled many times, though it took on its basic present shape in the 12th and 14th centuries. The castle is one of the three official residences of the Sovereign (the others are Buckingham Palace and Holyrood House, Edinburgh) and as such is in regular working use. In 1992 it suffered significant fire damage, but all areas have since been fully repaired and restored.

The most impressive of all the castle buildings is St George's Chapel, a masterpiece of English Gothic architecture, completed in 1511. Ten monarchs lie here, including Henry VIII and Charles I. The state apartments are hung with works from the Royal Collection, though the most startling exhibit is Queen Mary's dolls' house. Made in 1921 for the consort to King George V, it was designed in meticulous detail at one-twelfth life size with working plumbing and lifts, and miniature paintings and books donated by eminent writers and artists of the day.

Windsor town is a busy shopping centre but you can escape the crowds by exploring Windsor Park, a perfect place for a picnic. Close by, Legoland (➤ 111) makes a great day out for young children.

*Henry VIII's Gate, the main entrance to Windsor Castle; the famous king is also buried here*

# Where To...

221b Baker Street

Sherlock Holmes

"We met next day and inspected the rooms at 221b Baker Street....and at once entered into possession."

A STUDY IN SCARLET
Sir Arthur Conan Doyle

Above: at the
Tower of London
Right: Sherlock
Holmes' fictitious residence

# Central London

### Price rating

Approximate price for a three-course meal per person, excluding drinks:

£     = under £20
££    = £20–£30
£££   = over £30

Opting for the *prix fixe* menu (or set meal) at lunch time usually means prices are dramatically reduced – perhaps even halved.

Booking is essential for all higher-priced restaurants. Many of the places featured here are London's busiest restaurants – book as soon as you arrive in the capital, if not before. Smart casual dress is the norm (and often required) in more expensive places.

### Alastair Little (Soho) (£££)

Distinctive minimalist décor and fresh, light Modern European cooking from one of London's star chefs are the hallmarks of this famous Soho eatery. Book well in advance.
✉ 49 Frith Street, Soho
☎ 0171-734 5183 🕐 Lunch Mon–Fri, dinner Mon–Sat. Closed Sun 🚇 Leicester Square, Tottenham Court Road

### Al Bustan (££)

The name means garden in Arabic and greenery abounds in this classy, formal Lebanese restaurant, one of London's finest exponents of Middle Eastern cuisine.
✉ 27 Motcomb Street
☎ 0171-235 8277 🕐 Daily 12–11PM (last dinner)
🚇 Knightsbridge

### Aubergine (£££)

This tiny restaurant serves some of the best light Modern French cooking in London, and many would say the best food in the whole country. Book well in advance.
✉ 11 Park Walk, Chelsea SW10 ☎ 0171-352 3449
🕐 Lunch Mon–Fri, dinner Mon–Sat. Closed Sun, two weeks Christmas, first two weeks Aug 🚇 Sloane Square then 🚌 11, 19, 22, 211

### Bibendum (£££)

The splendid modern European brasserie-style food is probably the best of its kind in London and complements the brilliant Michelin art deco setting. Book well in advance.
✉ Michelin House, 81 Fulham Road, SW3 ☎ 0171-581 5817
🕐 Daily lunch, dinner
🚇 South Kensington

### Blakes (££)

Handy for Camden Market, this restaurant offers an interesting menu that meanders around the globe.
✉ 31 Jamestown Road
☎ 0171-482 2959 🕐 Daily lunch, dinner 🚇 Camden Town

### Bluebird (£££)

They don't come any trendier than this 'King's Road Gastrodome', which features a host of food shops as well as the centrepiece airy, light-filled restaurant. Superb Modern European cooking. Book well in advance.
✉ 350 King's Road, Chelsea
☎ 0171-559 1000 🕐 Daily lunch, dinner 🚇 Sloane Square then 🚌 19, 22 or 49

### Blues Bistro & Bar (£–££)

Trendy but not intimidating, with a small attractive dining room, serving serious Manhattan/European food at very reasonable prices.
✉ 42–3 Dean Street ☎ 0171-494 1966 🕐 Mon–Sat lunch, dinner Closed Sun
🚇 Leicester Square

### Butler's Wharf Chop House (£££)

Britannia rules the riverfront here with the very best of innovative Modern British cuisine. Lovely dining room but book a seat with a view to look on to Tower Bridge.
✉ Butler's Wharf Building, 36E Shad Thames ☎ 0171-403 3403
🕐 Mon–Fri lunch, dinner Closed lunch Sat, dinner Sun
🚇 Tower Hill, London Bridge

### Café-in-the-Crypt (£)

Dive beneath the Church of St Martin-in-the-Fields to find this oasis of calm amid the frenzy of Trafalgar Square.

Good salads, soups, sandwiches and light meals.

✉ Duncannon Street (Trafalgar Square) ☎ 0171-839 4342 🕐 Mon–Sat 10–8, Sun 12–8 🚇 Charing Cross, Leicester Square

### Café Pacifico (£)

This long-established Tex-Mex London institution is a cut above the average Margarita 'n' chilli joint.

✉ 5 Langley Street ☎ 0171-379 7728 🕐 Daily, 12–late 🚇 Covent Garden

### The Capital (£££)

Some of the best *haute cuisine* in town, expertly served in the decorous and elegant setting of the Capital Hotel.

✉ Basil Street, Knightsbridge ☎ 0171-589 5171 🕐 Daily lunch, dinner 🚇 Knightsbridge

### Le Caprice (£££)

It may be famous as the place where celebrities eat, but mere mortals also receive star treatment, and the food is excellent. Modern European cuisine. Timeless classic décor.

✉ Arlington House, Arlington Street ☎ 0171-629 2239 🕐 Daily lunch, dinner 🚇 Green Park

### Chelsea Bun Diner (£)

This long-established American-style café with a 200-item menu and typical US-size portions is one of Chelsea's few real bargains. All-day English breakfast and home-made pies also available.

✉ 9a Limerston Street ☎ 0171-352 3635 🕐 Daily, 7/8AM–midnight 🚇 Sloane Square then 🚌 11, 19, 22, 31

### Chez Gérard at the Opera Terrace (££)

The food doesn't always match the wonderful setting – a glass conservatory on top of Covent Garden's market

(book al-fresco if possible) – but the steak 'n' frites are usually excellent.

✉ First Floor, Opera Terrace, Covent Garden Central Market ☎ 0171-379 0666 🕐 Daily, 11AM–11:30PM (10:30 Sun) 🚇 Covent Garden

### Chez Nico at Ninety Park Lane (£££)

Nico Ladenis is one of the world's finest chefs and a meal here is as *haute* as *haute cuisine* goes. It's classic French with adroit touches from all over the world.

✉ 90 Park Lane ☎ 0171-409 1290 🕐 Lunch Mon–Fri, dinner Mon–Sat. Closed Sat lunch, all day Sun 🚇 Hyde Park Corner

### China City (£)

One of Chinatown's most attractive restaurants, with a lush fountain courtyard. The big draw is *dim sum*, though the full menu also proves good value.

✉ White Bear Yard, 25a Lisle Street ☎ 0171-734 3388 🕐 Mon–Sat noon–11:45PM Sun 11:30AM–11:15PM. 🚇 Leicester Square

### Connaught (£££)

Discreet, reserved and old-fashioned in the best sense, the classic French cooking here is impeccable. Traditional English dishes also appear at lunch time.

✉ Carlos Place ☎ 0171-499 7070 🕐 Daily lunch, dinner 🚇 Bond Street

### L'Escargot (ground floor ££, first floor £££)

This famous Soho establishment has been around since 1927 and despite ups and downs is back to its best with spot-on French/Mediterranean cooking.

✉ Greek Street ☎ 0171-437 6828 🕐 Ground floor lunch Mon–Fri, dinner Mon–Sat. Closed Sun. First floor closed Tue 🚇 Tottenham Court Rd

### Afternoon Tea

If you want to take afternoon tea in style try one of the following hotels: the Ritz, the Savoy, the Lanesborough, the Meridien Waldorf (where you are serenaded by a harpist), Brown's Hotel, Claridge's or the Dorchester. It's an expensive experience, but one you'll hopefully long treasure. Dress smartly (jacket and tie for men is the nominal code) and skip lunch beforehand! Other options (cheaper but still very classy) include Sotheby's and Fortnum & Mason.

### Chain Eating

There are a number of restaurant chains in London that provide inexpensive food of a consistently high standard. Probably the best is Pizza Express, with flagship branches at King's Road, Chelsea and at Dean Street, which is famous for its jazz. Other good cheap Italian options are Spaghetti House and Caffè Uno. Tasty brasserie chains include Chez Gérard (renowned for their steak'n'frites), Café Flo and Brown's.

### Gay Hussar (££)

London's favourite East European restaurant, and the haunt of literary and Bohemian types, has been going strong for over 45 years thanks largely to its good-value old-fashioned Hungarian cooking.

✉ 2 Greek Street ☎ 0171-437 0973 ⏱ Lunch daily, dinner Mon–Sat 🚇 Tottenham Court Road

### Greenhouse (££–£££)

Inventive modern British cooking in a spacious smart restaurant. Particularly popular at lunchtimes.

✉ 27a Hay's Mews ☎ 0171-499 3331 ⏱ Mon–Fri and Sun Lunch, daily dinner 🚇 Green Park, Hyde Park Corner

### The Ivy (£££)

One of London's most popular restaurants (book weeks ahead), this is a buzzing place where the Modern European cooking is wonderful.

✉ 1 West Street, Covent Garden ☎ 0171-836 4751 ⏱ Daily lunch, dinner 🚇 Leicester Square, Covent Garden

### Jason's Restaurant (£££)

Mauritian seafood by the Grand Union Canal in Little Venice is an unlikely prospect but works superbly well in this popular, cosmopolitan fish restaurant.

✉ opposite 60 Blomfield Road, Maida Vale ☎ 0171-286 6752 ⏱ Daily Lunch, Mon–Sat dinner Closed Sun dinner 🚇 Warwick Avenue

### Joe Allen (££)

Imaginative Californian-Italian cuisine on the edge of Covent Garden, but it's the celebrities and atmosphere that draws the crowds.

✉ 13 Exeter Street, Covent Garden ☎ 0171-836 0651 ⏱ Daily 11:30/12–late 🚇 Covent Garden

### Laicram Thai (££)

The menu covers the essential elements of Thai cuisine and waitresses in traditional costume add to the authentic atmosphere.

✉ 1 Blackheath Grove, Blackheath ☎ 0181-852 4710 ⏱ Tue–Sun lunch, dinner. Closed Mon, 🚇 Kew Gardens

### Lemonia (££)

You won't find Zorba's Dance or plate-smashing on the menu in this stylish Greek Cypriot establishment, often acclaimed as London's best Greek restaurant.

✉ 89 Regent's Park Road ☎ 0171-586 7454 ⏱ Mon–Fri and Sun lunch , Mon–Sat dinner 🚇 Chalk Farm

### Livebait (££)

Lively, informal seafood restaurant where the décor is simple and the standard of cooking and service is high.

✉ 43 The Cut ☎ 0171-928 7211 ⏱ Mon–Sat Lunch, dinner, Closed Sun 🚇 Waterloo

### Magic Wok (£)

Come here for an excellent range of Cantonese specials and friendly helpful service.

✉ 100 Queensway ☎ 0171-792 9767 ⏱ Daily 12–11PM 🚇 Queensway, Bayswater

### Mas Café (££)

Popular, informal neighbourhood hang-out with excellent Mediterranean- and North African-inspired cooking.

✉ 6–8 All Saints Road ☎ 0171-243 0969 ⏱ Daily Dinner, brunch only at weekends 🚇 Ladbroke Grove

### Matsuri (£££)

The ancient art of sushi meets the modern theatrics of teppenyaki in this colourful, festively decorated establishment.

✉ 15 Bury Street ☎ 0171-839 1101 ⏱ Mon–Sat lunch, dinner Closed Sun 🚇 Green Park, Piccadilly Circus

### Melati (£)

The doyen of London's Indonesian restaurants (Malaysian food also on offer), with excellent satays and some unusual dishes.

✉ 21 Great Windmill Street
☎ 0171-437 2745 🕐 Daily 12–late 🚇 Piccadilly Circus

### Le Meridien (£££)

A fabulous culinary experience, courtesy of Marco Pierre White – former *enfant terrible*, now probably the country's greatest chef.

✉ 21 Piccadilly ☎ 0171-734 8000 🕐 Daily lunch, dinner 🚇 Piccadilly Circus

### Museum Street Café (££)

Close to the British Museum, this is a small, simple operation offering fixed-price lunch and dinner menus featuring very good-value Modern European cuisine.

✉ 47 Museum Street
☎ 0171-405 3211 🕐 Tue–Fri Lunch , Mon–Fri dinner . Closed Sat–Sun 🚇 Holborn, Tottenham Court Road

### Navarro's Tapas Bar (£)

Some of London's best *tapas* as well as a short menu of full traditional Spanish meals, served in an attractive tiled dining room.

✉ 67 Charlotte Street
☎ 0171-637 7713 🕐 Mon–Fri lunch , Mon–Sat dinner. Closed Sun 🚇 Goodge Street

### October Gallery Café (£)

This charming gallery-cum-café is a must for impoverished hungry artists. Eat in the pine-clad dining room in winter, in the small courtyard in summer. Both art and food are eclectic.

✉ 24 Old Gloucester Street
☎ 0171-242 7367 🕐 12:30–2:30 Tue–Sat 🚇 Holborn

### Odette's (££–£££)

Charming romantic restaurant serving superb innovative Modern European dishes. For a taste of the same at lower prices try the basement wine bar.

✉ 130 Regent's Park Road
☎ 0171-586 5486
🕐 Restaurant: lunch Mon–Fri, dinner Mon–Sat. Wine bar: lunch Daily dinner Mon–Sat. Closed Sun 🚇 Chalk Farm

### Paris–London Café (£)

In an unappealing position opposite Archway tube (handy for Highgate), this simple unpretentious café owned by two French brothers turns out superb, homely, award-winning French cooking.

✉ 3 Junction Road ☎ 0171-561 0330 🕐 9AM–11PM Mon–Sat. Closed Sun 🚇 Archway

### Poons

A Chinatown legend, Poons is famous for its scruffy, cramped conditions, rude staff and above all its air-dried meats. Forewarned is forearmed this Soho institution is still well worth a visit!

✉ 4 Leicester Street ☎ 0171-437 1528 🕐 Daily 12–11:30 🚇 Leicester Square

### Quaglino's (£££)

Despite a dining room that seats 267 and resembles an ocean liner there's a real buzz to this trendy theatrical restaurant. Good Modern European cuisine in a very French bistro/brasserie atmosphere.

✉ 16 Bury Street ☎ 0171-930 6767 🕐 Daily 12 until late 🚇 Green Park

### The Ritz (£££)

A byword for style and elegance, the cooking may not quite match the fabulous setting and service but opt for the set lunch and you won't go too far wrong.

✉ 150 Piccadilly ☎ 0171-493 8181 🕐 Mon–Sat lunch, dinner Sun Lunch only 🚇 Green Park

### Themes and Gimmicks

The Hard Rock Café started it all in 1971, now Planet Hollywood (at the Trocadero) is competing for top billing, while near by on Shaftesbury Avenue is the jungle of the Rainforest Café. Off-the-wall oddities include Garlic & Shots (Frith Street, Soho), a Swedish concept whereby everything (yes, everything) comes with garlic; Sarastro – The Show after the Show, Drury Lane, Covent Garden, which may appeal to operatic luvvies; and best/worst of all, the Elvis Graceland Palace on the Old Kent Road (☎ 0171-639 3961), a little way out of the centre, but a real experience!

## Pie and Mash

The nearest London comes to indigenous restaurants is the famed Pie and Mash shops. The filling in the pie used to be eels, but nowadays these are only served stewed or in aspic as jellied eels. The standard pie filling is now minced beef and the meal comes with a green sauce or gravy known as 'liquor', made from parsley. Sadly, only a few shops remain, but Cockneys Pie and Mash, Portobello Road, by the market; R Cook, The Cut, behind Waterloo Station; and Goddard's Ye Old Pie House at Greenwich are all worth a visit.

## Rock and Sole Plaice (£)

A visit to this long-established fish-and-chip shop-cum-restaurant makes a good interlude, or finale, to a night of drinking in Covent Garden.
✉ 47 Endell Street ☎ 0171-836 3785 🕐 Eat-in 11:30–10 (9PM Sun). Takeaway 11:30AM–11:30pm (10PM Sun)
🚇 Covent Garden

## Rules (£££)

London's oldest restaurant celebrated 200 years trading in 1998 (here Dickens ate and Edward VII and Lillie Langtry held lovers' trysts) and still draws plaudits for its top-quality quintessential British food.
✉ 34 Maiden Lane, Covent Garden ☎ 0171-836 5314 🕐 Daily lunch, dinner 🚇 Covent Garden, Charing Cross

## Soho Spice (£)

Limited but high-quality menu. And when you see your bill you may well agree with the claim that this is the best-value Indian restaurant in Soho.
✉ 124–26 Wardour Street ☎ 0171-434 0808 🕐 7:30AM–12AM Mon–Fri, 12–12 Sat. Closed Sun 🚇 Leicester Square, Tottenham Court Road

## Stephen Bull, W1 (£££)

A pioneer of Modern British cooking, this is the eponymous star chef's original, award-winning restaurant. Inspirations come mostly from northern Europe and the Mediterranean.
✉ 5–7 Blandford Street ☎ 0171-486 9696 🕐 Lunch Mon–Fri, dinner Mon–Sat. Closed Sun 🚇 Baker Street, Bond Street

## Sweetings (££)

A time-warp tourist attraction in its own right, Sweetings (established here in 1906) is one of London's oldest fish and oyster restaurants.
✉ 39 Queen Victoria Street, The City ☎ 0171-248 3062 (no bookings) 🕐 Mon–Fri 11:30–3 🚇 Cannon Street

## La Tante Claire (£££)

The grand old dame of French cuisine in the capital, three-star chef Pierre Koffman serves up an unbeatable experience. Book well in advance.
✉ 68 Royal Hospital Road ☎ 0171-352 6045 🕐 Mon–Fri lunch, dinner 🚇 Sloane Square

## The Well (£)

Drop into The Well for reliable home-made food and particularly nice cakes.
✉ 2 Ecclestone Place ☎ 0171-730 7303 🕐 Mon–Sat 9–5:30 🚇 Victoria

## Veronica's (££)

The fascinating award-winning menu here is a history lesson in British cooking with replication or adaptations of recipes going back 600 years. Fortunately it works brilliantly!
✉ 3 Hereford Road ☎ 0171-229 5079 🕐 Lunch Mon–Fri, dinner Mon–Sat. Closed Sun 🚇 Bayswater, Queensway

## Zafferano (££)

One of central London's very best Italian restaurants, Zafferano is often packed with celebrities but remains unpretentious with the cooking being the main attraction.
✉ 15 Lowndes Street ☎ 0171-235 5800 🕐 Mon–Sat lunch, dinner 🚇 Knightsbridge

# Pubs & Wine Bars

### Cork and Bottle
Typical old-fashioned London basement wine-bar, very popular early evening; go later to avoid the crush.
✉ **44–6 Cranbourne Street**
☎ **0171-734 7807** 🕐 **Daily all day** 🚇 **Leicester Square**

### The Eagle
An award-winning crowd-puller, popular with media types. Serves probably the best pub food (mostly Mediterranean) in London.
✉ **159 Farringdon Road**
☎ **0171-837 1353**
🕐 **Mon–Sat 12–11; lunch 12–2:30; dinner 6:30–10:30**
🚇 **Farringdon**

### French House
This unusual pub has been a Soho institution for over 80 years. One for Francophiles, gourmets and wine-lovers, this is no place for beer drinkers but there is an excellent restaurant upstairs.
✉ **49 Dean Street**
☎ **0171-437 2477** 🕐 **Daily 12–11 (Sun 10:30)**
🚇 **Leicester Square**

### The George Inn
London's only remaining galleried inn is a survivor from 1677, and during the summer Shakespeare's plays are performed in the courtyard. Owned by the National Trust.
✉ **George Inn Yard**
☎ **0171-407 2056** 🕐 **Daily**
🚇 **London Bridge**

### Gordon's
Dip into the vaults of London's most atmospheric wine bar for a trip back to the 18th century.
✉ **47 Villiers Street**
☎ **0171-930 1408** 🕐 **Mon–Fri 11–11 Sat 5–11 Closed Sun**
🚇 **Embankment**

### The Holly Bush
Hidden away in a corner of old Hampstead, this simple, wood-panelled pub is a favourite retreat when city crowds get too oppressive.
✉ **22 Holly Mount, off Heath St, Hampstead** ☎ **0171-435 2892**
🕐 **Mon–Fri 12–3, 5:30–11, (Sat 12–11, Sun 12–10:30**
🚇 **Hampstead**

### Lamb and Flag
Covent Garden's most characterful and atmospheric historic pub, tucked away in a small alleyway.
✉ **33 Rose Street** ☎ **0171-497 9504** 🕐 **Mon–Sat 11–11, Sun 12–10:30** 🚇 **Leicester Square**

### The Lamb
Splendid 18th-century pub with much of its original bar woodwork and glass, including rare swivel glass 'snob screens'.
✉ **Lamb's Conduit**
☎ **0171-405 0713** 🕐 **Daily**
🚇 **Russell Square**

### Ye Olde Cheshire Cheese
Essentially unchanged since 1667, the Cheshire Cheese is one of London's oldest and certainly most atmospheric pubs. Try their famous steak and kidney pudding.
✉ **Wine Office Court, 145 Fleet Street** ☎ **0171-353 6170**
🕐 **Closed Sun eve**
🚇 **Chancery Lane, Blackfriars**

### Prospect of Whitby
London's quintessential river pub, built in 1520, was patronised by Dickens, Turner and Whistler.
✉ **57 Wapping Wall** ☎ **0171-481 1095** 🕐 **Mon–Fri, 11:30AM–3PM, 5:30PM–11PM. Sat 11:30–11, Sun 12–10:30**
🚇 **Wapping**

### Meals with a View
If you want to look down on London from your dining table the best place is the eighth-storey Oxo Tower Restaurant (➤ 63). There are more riverside views from Butler's Wharf Chop House (➤ 92), the People's Palace in the Royal Festival Hall on the South Bank and the Blueprint Café at the Design Museum (➤ 39). For a different perspective, ascend to the Fifth Floor Café at Harvey Nichol's (➤ 107) or zoom up 28 floors to The Windows, at the Hilton Hotel on Park Lane.

# Outer London & Beyond

## Vegetarian Options

Vegetarians in London need not worry as there are interesting meat-free dishes on most good restaurant menus. Vegetarian heaven is to be found in Neal's Yard (Covent Garden ➤ 38), where there is a clutch of excellent wholefood restaurants, cafés and shops. Off here, on Neal Street, Food for Thought is recommended. Another good option is to try one of London's many Indian restaurants, particularly Woodlands, with branches at 77 Marylebone Lane and 37 Panton Street, off Leicester Square.

## Outer London

### Greenwich

#### Goddard's Ye Old Pie House (£)

The décor doesn't come much more basic than in this long-established pie restaurant but you won't taste a better steak and kidney pie in London.

✉ 45 Greenwich Church Street ☎ No phone ⏰ Jul–Sep Tue–Fri, Sun 11–3 (closed Mon), Sat 10:45–4:30; Oct–Jun Wed–Fri, Sun 11–3 (closed Mon, Tue) Sat 10:45–4:30 🚊 Greenwich Pier 🚇 Island Gardens then foot tunnel 🚉 Greenwich

#### Spread Eagle (££)

Good French food in an old coaching inn, next to Greenwich Theatre. Charming courtyard.

✉ 1–2 Stockwell Street ☎ 0181-853 2333 ⏰ Lunch daily 12–2:30, dinner Mon–Sat 6:30–10:30 🚊 Greenwich Pier 🚇 Island Gardens then foot tunnel 🚉 Greenwich

### Hampton Court

#### Monsieur Max (£–££)

Renowned for its excellent *cuisine bourgeoisie* served by the eponymous owner-chef. Set menus only.

✉ 133 High Street, Hampton Hill ☎ 0181-979 5546 🚉 Kew Gardens then 🚌 68.

### Kew

#### The Original Maids of Honour (£)

One of London's most famous tea rooms, renowned for its delicious Maids of Honour cakes. Meals too.

✉ 288 Kew Road (opposite Cumberland Gate, Kew Gardens) ☎ 0181-940 2752 ⏰ Mon 9–1,

Tue–Sat 9:30–6 (lunch 12:30–2:30). Closed Sun 🚉 Kew Gardens

#### Wine and Moussaka (£)

Hearty Greek food in an informal setting. Garden.

✉ 12 Kew Green ☎ 0181-940 5696 ⏰ Mon–Sat Lunch, dinner Closed Sun 🚉 Kew Gardens

### Richmond

#### Beeton's (£)

All-day informal eating. Mostly British menu but other interesting dishes usually on offer. Unlicensed, so bring your own alcohol.

✉ 58 Hill Rise ☎ 0181-940 9561 ⏰ Lunch 12–4 Sat, Sun; dinner 6–10 Tue–Sun 🚉 Richmond

#### Chez Lindsay (£)

Breton seafood and pancakes are the specialities of this cosy French bistro-restaurant.

✉ 11 Hill Rise ☎ 0181-948 7473 ⏰ Mon–Sat 11–11, Sun 12–10 🚉 Richmond

## Outside London

### Bath

#### The Hole in the Wall (££)

This famous, long-established cosy basement restaurant was pivotal in the development of new British cuisine.

✉ 16 George Street ☎ 01225-425 242 ⏰ Daily, lunch, dinner

#### Moon and Sixpence (£)

Set in the old main post office serving excellent-value lunches and dinners. Conservatory and courtyard for summer dining.

✉ 6A Broad Street ☎ 01225-460962 ⏰ Daily, 12–2:30 (Sat 3), 5:30 (Sun 7)–10:30/11

### The Pump Room (£–££)

Built in 1795, the decadently grand Pump Room was once the social heart of the spa city and is still an enormously popular place. Here you can taste the spa water and take the traditional lunch or tea.

✉ **Stall Street (part of the Roman Baths complex)**
☎ **01225-444477** 🕐 **Daily 9:30–4:30, lunch 12–2:30**

### Sally Lunn's (£)

Savour the atmosphere of Bath's oldest house, built in 1482, while tucking into the original famous (brioche-like) Bath Bun. Full meals also served.

✉ **4 North Parade Passage**
☎ **01225-461634**
🕐 **Restaurant open Tue–Sun 10AM–11PM, Sun 11–11**

## Cambridge
### Free Press(£)

In a back street not far from the city centre this, traditional town pub was named after a local 19th-century pro-temperance journal. Now serves interesting food and good real ale.

✉ **Prospect Row**
☎ **01223-368337** 🕐 **Daily 12–2:30, 6–11**

### Little Tea Room at Perfect Setting (£)

Set in a whitewashed Georgian house, this really is the perfect place for an all-day breakfast, traditional afternoon tea or a sandwich at any time.

✉ **All Saints Passage**
☎ **01223-63207** 🕐 **Mon–Sat 9:30–5:30, Sun 12–5:30**

### Midsummer House (£££)

Victorian villa on the Riverside serving modern British/European fare.

✉ **Midsummer Common**
☎ **01223-369 299** 🕐 **Tue–Fri, Sun 12:30–1:45 (last lunch); Tue–Sat 7:30–10 (last dinner). Closed lunch Sat, Mon; dinner Sun, Mon**

## Oxford
### Brown's (£)

Buzzing, informal restaurant with a wide range of popular dishes from sandwiches to more serious food.

✉ **5 Woodstock Road**
☎ **01865-311415** 🕐 **Mon–Sat 11AM–11:30PM, Sun 12–11:30**

### Nosebag (£)

Homemade quiches, salads, soups and sandwiches plus imaginative daily special dishes have students and visitors queuing at this attractive restaurant.

✉ **6 St Michael's Street**
☎ **01865-721033**
🕐 **Daily from 9:30; closes Mon 5:30, Tue–Thu 10, Fri–Sat 10:30, Sun 9**

### Le Petit Blanc (££)

Owned by culinary maestro Raymond Blanc, but with prices which won't make grown men weep, this is a splendid taste of Modern European cooking in a stylish, cosmopolitan, town centre brasserie.

✉ **71–2 Walton Street**
☎ **01865-510 999**
🕐 **Daily, lunch, dinner**

## Windsor
### The Castle Hotel (£££)

In the regal shadow of Windsor's great castle, the popular and inventive restaurant combines traditional themes with modern culinary ideas.

✉ **High Street, Windsor**
☎ **01753-851011** 🕐 **Daily, 12:00–2:, 7–10:00**

### Eton Wine Bar (£)

Book a riverside conservatory table at this perennially popular wine bar just over the footbridge spanning the Thames, dividing Windsor and Eton. Good inventive menu and very reasonable wine prices.

✉ **High Street, Eton**
☎ **01753-854921** 🕐 **Daily, 12–2:30, 6–10:30 (Sat 11)**

### Cream Tea

Try to take an early lunch when making an excursion out of London in order to leave time and space for that most English of institutions, the cream tea. Not so fussy or substantial as formal afternoon tea (► 61) a traditional cream tea comprises a pot of tea with two scones, cream and strawberry jam. It's often too much for one person so you may want to share the scones.

# Central London

## Hotel Prices

All prices are for one night's double room, whatever the occupancy – though American visitors should note that it is rare for a whole family to be allowed to share.

£ = £45–£70
££ = £70–£150
£££ = over £150

## Athenaeum (£££)

This elegant hotel over-looking Green Park remains one of the most popular and friendly in the area. Lovely bedrooms and a spa for the exclusive use of guests.
✉ Piccadilly ☎ 0171-499 3464; fax 0171-493 1860 🚇 Green Park

## Avonmore Hotel (£–££)

A privately owned award-winning B&B with just nine bedrooms and a friendly atmosphere.
✉ 66 Avonmore Road, Kensington ☎ 0171-603 3121; fax 0171-603 4035 🚇 West Kensington

## Beaufort (£££)

This small award-winning hotel, situated in a quiet tree-lined square near Harrods, is comfortably furnished with lots of individual extras.
✉ 33 Beaufort Gardens ☎ 0171-584 5252; fax 0171-589 2834 🚇 Knightsbridge

## The Berkeley (£££)

In an enviable situation with views over the greenery of Hyde Park, this traditional hotel offers exemplary standards of accommodation and service. It boasts beautiful rooms and first-class leisure facilities.
✉ Wilton Place, Knightsbridge ☎ 0171-235 6000; fax 0171-235 4330 🚇 Knightsbridge

## Brown's (£££)

Tucked away in the heart of Mayfair, Brown's is the epitome of traditional English elegance with an atmos-phere of discreet exclusivity.
✉ Albemarle Street/Dover Street ☎ 0171-493 6020; fax 0171-493 9381 🚇 Green Park

## Byron (££)

A charming terraced house, thoughtfully restored. Bedrooms are comfortable and tastefully furnished.
✉ 36-38 Queensborough Terrace ☎ 0171-243 0987; fax 0171-792 1957 🚇 Queensway

## Capital (£££)

Small and exclusive, the Capital, set in the heart of Knightsbridge, attracts a loyal clientele. Superb restaurant (► 93).
✉ Basil Street ☎ 0171-589 5171; fax 0171-225 0011 🚇 Knightsbridge

## Claridge's (£££)

A London institution welcoming royalty and heads of state for almost a century. Supremely comfortable bedrooms and opulent public areas.
✉ Brook Street ☎ 0171-629 8860; fax 0171-499 2210 🚇 Bond Street

## Comfort Inn, Hampstead (££)

Friendly hotel close to Hampstead Heath; popular with overseas visitors. Bedrooms are thoughtfully equipped, and the public rooms are bright and comfortable.
✉ 5–7 Frognal, Hampstead ☎ 0171-794 0101; fax 0171-794 0100 🚇 Hampstead

## Comfort Inn, Kensington (££)

Very conveniently located for access to Earl's Court, this cheerful modern hotel offers smart bedrooms and friendly service.
✉ 22-32 West Cromwell Road, Kensington ☎ 0171-373 3300; fax 0171-835 2040 🚇 Earl's Court

## Connaught (£££)

Perhaps the most discreet and reserved of London's great hotels, the Connaught retains its century-old atmosphere. Recently updated without compromising its quiet luxury.

✉ **Carlos Place** ☎ **0171-499 7070; fax 0171-495 3262** Ⓤ **Bond Street**

## Delmere (££)

Smart friendly staff, well-equipped rooms, a jazz-themed bar and particularly comfortable lounge are the main attractions of this fine hotel near Hyde Park.

✉ **130 Sussex Gardens** ☎ **0171-706 3344; fax 0171-262 1863** Ⓤ **Paddington**

## Dorchester (£££)

Undoubtedly one of the world's finest hotels. The beautifully furnished bedrooms with sumptuous bathrooms have become a hallmark.

✉ **Park Lane** ☎ **0171-629 8888; fax 0171-409 0114** Ⓤ **Hyde Park Corner**

## Goring (£££)

Among London's most famous quality small hotels, the Goring provides a wonderful example of good old-fashioned British hospitality and service.

✉ **Beeston Place, Grosvenor Gardens** ☎ **0171-396 9000; fax 0171-834 4393** Ⓤ **Victoria**

## Halkin (£££)

One of the more individual-istic of London's top hotels, with classically influenced, Italian-designed public areas and striking bedrooms.

✉ **Halkin Street, Belgravia** ☎ **0171-333 1000; fax 0171-333 1100** Ⓤ **Hyde Park Corner**

## Hart House Hotel (££)

This elegant Georgian town house is part of a terrace of mansions which were home to French nobility during the French Revolution. Sympathetically restored and run by the owner.

✉ **51 Gloucester Place, Portman Square** ☎ **0171-935 2288; fax 0171-935 8516** Ⓤ **Baker Street**

## Ibis Euston (£)

Bright, well-maintained bedrooms, a public bar-lounge and a secure covered car park make this popular hotel good value for its central location, near Euston station.

✉ **3 Cardington Street** ☎ **0171-388 7777; fax 0171-388 0001** Ⓤ **Euston**

## Kingsway (£–££)

This owner-managed 29-bedroom hotel is situated in a quiet landscaped garden square close to Hyde Park.

✉ **27 Norfolk Square** ☎ **0171-723 5569; fax 0171-723 7317** Ⓤ **Paddington**

## Lanesborough (£££)

Famous London landmark on Hyde Park Corner with superbly appointed, thought-fully equipped bedrooms, and butlers to offer the highest standards of personal service. Popular cocktail bar.

✉ **Hyde Park Corner** ☎ **0171-259 5599; fax 0171-259 5606** Ⓤ **Hyde Park Corner**

## London County Hall Travel Inn Capital (£)

A large city centre hotel that offers smart, spacious and well-equipped bedrooms, ideally suited for use by families.

✉ **Belvedere Road** ☎ **01582-414341** Ⓤ **Waterloo**

## Hotel Ratings

Most hotel rates are inclusive of all taxes, service charges and breakfast, which usually means full English breakfast (▶ 61), though do check this. Perversely, only the most expensive hotels have the temerity to charge extra for breakfast.

## On a Budget

Travellers on a wafer-thin budget should consider staying at one of London's 18 YMCA/YWCA hostels or at one of the seven YHA hostels. The YHA hostels in particular are extremely good value and in surprisingly central locations, consequently you'll generally need to book at least three months ahead for the summer. Contact the YMCA/YWCA at 640 Forest Road E17 ☎ 0181-520 5599, and the YHA, 8 St Stephen's Hill, St Alban's, Herts AL1 2DY ☎ 01727-855215. London Tourist Board offices can help with other student, youth and group accommodation.

## London Tourist Hotel (£)

A small bed and breakfast hotel, newly refurbished, with 32 bedrooms. All en-suite and with colour television and telephone.

✉ 15 Penywern Road, Earl's Court ☎ 0171-370 4356; fax 0171-370 7923 🚇 Earl's Court

## Mandarin Oriental, Hyde Park (£££)

Once used as residential chambers for Victorian gentlemen, this traditional building has been thoroughly updated with individually decorated and spacious rooms.

✉ 66 Knightsbridge ☎ 0171-235 2000; fax 0171-235 4552 🚇 Knightsbridge

## Le Meridien Piccadilly (£££)

For many, this well-established luxury hotel lies at the very hub of London life. Among its many boasts is star chef Marco Pierre White (► 95).

✉ 21 Piccadilly ☎ 0171-734 8000; fax 0171-437 3574 🚇 Piccadilly Circus

## Le Meridien Waldorf (£££)

The Waldorf goes from strength to strength with a recent injection of enthusiastic and committed managerial staff. The Palm Court Lounge is a London legend.

✉ Aldwych ☎ 0171-836 2400; fax 0171-836 7244 🚇 Charing Cross

## Mitre House Hotel (££)

A long-established family-run hotel with 70 rooms, all en-suite and with good facilities, close to Hyde Park.

✉ 178–84 Sussex Gardens ☎ 0171-723 8040; fax 0171-402 0990 🚇 Lancaster Gate

## Norfolk Plaza (££)

This comfortable hotel is located in a quiet residential square and within easy walking distance of the West End.

✉ 29-33 Norfolk Square, Paddington ☎ 0171-723 0792; fax 0171-224 8770 🚇 Paddington

## The Ritz (£££)

A London legend with a reputation that stretches around the globe. The sumptuous bedrooms are furnished in Louis XVI style and the public rooms are palatial (► 95).

✉ 150 Piccadilly ☎ 0171-493 8181; fax 0171-493 2687 🚇 Green Park

## The Savoy (£££)

Another London institution. High standards of comfort and quality with many of its famous features preserved, including the art deco styling.

✉ Strand ☎ 0171-836 4343; fax 0171-240 6040 🚇 Charing Cross

## Stafford (£££)

Tucked away in exclusive St James, the Stafford represents the height of luxury. Elegant, individually designed bedrooms and beautiful public areas.

✉ 16–18 St James's Place ☎ 0171-493 0111; fax 0171-493 7121 🚇 Green Park

## Swiss House Hotel (£–££)

Comfortable, well-situated 16-room hotel in a pretty, residential area of South Kensington, convenient for museums and shopping.

✉ 171 Old Brompton Road ☎ 0171-373 2769; fax 0171 373 4983 🚇 South Kensington

# Central London & Excursions

### Tower Thistle (£££)
A great location next to the Tower of London with wonderful views of Tower Bridge and St Katharine's Dock is the attraction of this large, busy, modern hotel.

✉ St Katharine's Way
☎ 0171-481 2575; fax 0171-488 4106 🚇 Tower Hill

### Wigmore Court(£-££)
Conveniently positioned with bright and welcoming public areas and equally appealing bedrooms.

✉ 23 Gloucester Place
☎ 0171-935 0928; fax 0171-487 4259 🚇 Baker Street

## Outside London

## Bath
### Bath Tasburgh (£–££)
Set in an acre of beautifully tended gardens this charming Victorian House enjoys glorious views over the Avon Valley. The adjacent canal towpath provides an idyllic walk into town.

✉ Warminster Road
☎ 01225-425096, fax 01225 463842

### Haringtons (££)
Located in a picturesque cobbled city-centre street this friendly relaxed hotel offers a high standard of modern comforts within a distinctive 18th-century building.

✉ 8–10 Queen Street
☎ 01225-461728, fax 01225-444804

## Cambridge
### Arundel House (£–££)
Just a short walk from the city centre, the Arundel looks out onto the river and open parkland. Its Victorian conservatory with an all-day lounge menu is a delightful place to sit and relax. Ask for the bedrooms in the converted coach house.

✉ Chesterton Road
☎ 01223-367701, fax 01223-367721

## Oxford
### The Randolph (£££)
This famous landmark hotel in the centre of Oxford has a timeless elegance and features many superb architectural features.

✉ Beaumont Street
☎ 01865-247481, fax 01865-791678

### The Eastgate (££)
A relaxing English country house-style hotel, ideally situated at the heart of this historic city centre close to the Thames and Magdalen Bridge.

✉ The High, at the corner of Merton Street ☎ 01865-248244, fax 01865-791681

## Windsor
### Ye Harte and Garter (£–££)
This extended Victorian building enjoys exciting views of the imposing Windsor Castle and offers high standards of accommodation as well as a wide range of dining options.

✉ High Street ☎ 01753-863426, fax 01753-830527

### Aurora Garden (££)
Small friendly hotel set in a residential neighbourhood a few minutes stroll from the town centre. The cooking is very good and diners look out onto the hotel's pride and joy, a landscaped water garden.

✉ Bolton Avenue
☎ 01753-868686, fax 01753-831394

### Booking a Bed
If you arrive in London without accommodation, don't worry. You can make same-day bookings at the tourist information centres at Victoria Station, Liverpool Street Station, Heathrow Airport, Selfridges and the EuroStar terminal at Waterloo station. There is a small charge for this service.

# Shopping Areas

## Shop Opening Times

Traditionally London shop opening hours have been Monday to Saturday 9:30–6. Many West End stores stay open later on Thursdays; in Knightsbridge late night is Wednesdays. More recently, however, several shops are opening later at other times and also on Sunday (from 11 or noon). If opening times are not indicated in the entry then you can assume that they operate more-or-less traditional hours. In tourist enclaves such as Covent Garden, Sunday opening is the norm.

## Bond Street

London's most exclusive shopping street is expensive for buying, but a great place for just looking. *Haute couture*, antiques, auction houses, fine-art galleries and jewellers predominate.

🚇 **Green Park, Bond Street**

## Charing Cross Road

A bookworm's heaven, for both new and used books. For general browsing try Blackwells, Book Etc, Foyles (▶ 105) or Waterstones. For specialist, second-hand and antiquarian books, Cecil Court, off Charing Cross Road, is a gem.

🚇 **Leicester Square, Tottenham Court Road**

## Covent Garden–Neal Street

Specialism is the key here with The Kite Store, The Hat Shop, The Bead Shop, and many other one-off stars. Neal's Yard attracts wholefood lovers, while young shoppers come for the high fashion on Short's Gardens.

🚇 **Covent Garden**

## Covent Garden Piazza

Lots of small, individual, often idiosyncratic, shops in a buzzing traffic-free environment.

🚇 **Covent Garden**

## Jermyn Street

Both a historical attraction and a shopping street, Jermyn Street is London shopping at its old-fashioned best. (▶ 48)

🚇 **Green Park,**

## Kensington

Cheap and retro clothing can be found at Kensington Market, antiques and art abound on up-market Kensington Church Street, and behind the beautiful art deco front of Barkers is a good department store.

🚇 **Kensington High Street**

## King's Road

Birthplace of the mini-skirt and the Punk movement, the King's Road is still up-to-the-minute on street fashion, but is less radical these days. This is also a good place to buy antiques and curios.

🚇 **Sloane Square**

## Oxford Street

London's most frenetic shopping street presents a cocophony of global styles and noise and is generally only worth patronising for its department stores. However, off here at St Christopher's Place and South Molton Street (immediately north and south of Bond Street tube respectively) are some cutting-edge designer-fashion outlets.

🚇 **Marble Arch, Bond Street, Oxford Circus, Tottenham Court Rd**

## Regent Street

A handsome boulevard with many exclusive shops including gold, silver and jewellery at Mappin & Webb and Garrard & Co; toys at Hamley's (▶ 111), and Liberty (▶ 107).

🚇 **Oxford Circus**

## Sloane Street

Armani, Chanel, Dior, Lacroix, D&G, Hermès, Katharine Hamnett, Prada, Roland Klein, Valentino are just some of the designer names to be found here.

🚇 **Sloane Square (south end), Knightsbridge (north end)**

# Antiques & Books

## Antiques

### Alfie's Antique Market
Great for looking as well as buying, Alfie's is a London institution. Don't miss the post-war kitchenware in the basement!
✉ 13–25 Church Street
☎ 0171-723 6066 🚇 Edgware Road, Marylebone Road

### Antiquarius
This attractive up-market Chelsea arcade holds around 120 dealers covering a wide range of wares.
✉ 131–41 King's Road
☎ 0171-351 5353 🚇 Sloane Square then 🚌 11, 19 or 22

### Bermondsey (New Caledonian) Market
London's prime market for serious antiques collectors and the trade, who snap up most of the bargains shortly after the horribly early opening hour of 5AM.
✉ Bermondsey Square
🕐 Fri 5AM–2PM (starts closing at 12) 🚇 London Bridge

### Camden Passage
Confusingly located not in Camden, but in trendy Islington, with one of the biggest concentration of antiques in the whole country. Dozens of high-quality dealers but few bargains.
✉ off Upper Street ☎ 0171-359 9969 🚇 Angel

### Chelsea Antiques Market
Claimed to be the oldest antiques market in Britain, the dealers here cover most interests and at prices that are relatively good value compared to the Kings Road.
✉ 245a–253 King's Road
☎ 0171-352 5689 🚇 Sloane Square

### Portobello Road
(Markets, ➤ 108–9)

## Books

### Any Amount of Books
You'll find thousands of second-hand general-interest volumes here, and they are well ordered so that browsing is a pleasure instead of a chore.
✉ 62 Charing Cross Road
☎ 0171-240 8140
🚇 Leicester Square

### Dillons
Probably the best alternative to Foyles (➤ below) for that elusive volume. Good second-hand department.
✉ 82 Gower Street ☎ 0171-636 1577 🕐 Daily
🚇 Tottenham Court Rd

### Forbidden Planet
The extraterrestrial monsters in the window tell you what to expect at this sci-fi/fantasy mecca. Videos, toys, comics and magazines too. A good place to take the kids.
✉ 71–75 New Oxford Street
☎ 0171-836 4179
🚇 Tottenham Court Road

### Foyles
Despite its apparent disorder, this is the biggest book shop in Britain so you're sure to find what you want here – eventually.
✉ 113–119 Charing Cross Road
☎ 0171-437 5660
🚇 Tottenham Court Rd

### Stanford's
The world's largest travel book shop with a vast selection of guides, travelogues and maps to everywhere on earth.
✉ 12–14 Long Acre ☎ 0171-836 1915 🚇 Leicester Square

### Presents from the Past
Some of the best high-quality individual souvenirs and gifts are to be found in museum shops. You don't have to pay to get in as they are outside the turnstiles, or you will be issued with a special (free) ticket. The British Museum, the South Kensington museums and the Design Museum are particularly noteworthy, while The Museum Store at 37 The Market, Covent Garden Piazza, goes a step further, trawling the best of the world's museums for ideas.

# Clothing, Cosmetics & Department Stores

## London's Arcades

American cities have shopping malls, London has arcades. These covered walkways full of small individual shops, many of which are jewellers and antiques dealers, provide a fascinating glimpse into the past. The best example is Burlington Arcade (off Piccadilly), built in 1819, where beadles in top hats and great coats still ensure that decorum is maintained. Directly opposite, running down to Jermyn Street, is Piccadilly Arcade and just around the corner, connecting Old Bond Street to Albemarle Street, is Royal Arcade. Also off Jermyn Street is Princes Arcade.

## Clothing and Accessories

### Aquascutum
Top-quality traditional British rainwear (often useful in London), accessories, and other mid-price clothing for the discerning shopper.
✉ **100 Regent Street** ☎ **0171-734 6090** Ⓟ **Piccadilly Circus**

### Bates the Hatter
London's favourite hat shop has been topping off the famous (and not-so-famous) since 1902 in panamas, trilbys, top hats and the like. A joy to visit.
✉ **21a Jermyn Street**
☎ **0171-734 2722**
Ⓟ **Piccadilly Circus**

### Brown's
One of London's best designer boutiques claiming the biggest range of labels. For discount gear try their branch Brown's Labels for Less, just a few yards away at 50 South Molton Street.
✉ **23–7 South Molton Street**
☎ **0171-491 7833** Ⓟ **Bond Street**

### Burberry's
The famous Burberry check is not just confined to trenchcoats and scarves. Choose from over 300 lines at this very British institution.
✉ **18–22 Haymarket** ☎ **0171-930 3343** Ⓟ **Piccadilly Circus**

### Fenwick
If you're in Bond Street but don't want to go in the designer boutiques, this unintimidating department store carries many of the same names.
✉ **63 New Bond Street**
☎ **0171-629 9161** Ⓟ **Bond Street**

### Laura Ashley
Typecast as the quintessential English rose, Laura Ashley has been revamped to include more daring modern fashions. There are several branches throughout London.
✉ **256–8 Regent Street**
☎ **0171-437 9760** Ⓟ **Oxford Circus**

### Lillywhite's
The last name in branded sports clothing, with traditional British sports best represented though you will find there is stock from all over the world.
✉ **24–36 Lower Regent Street**
☎ **0171-915 4000** Ⓒ **Daily**
Ⓟ **Piccadilly Circus**

### Paul Smith
One of Britain's most successful designers, Paul Smith takes classics and adds a twist or two. Large range at this branch – try the big department stores, too.
✉ **40–44 Floral Street**
☎ **0171-379 7133** Ⓟ **Covent Garden**

### Scotch House
Three floors of traditional Scottish tartans and woollens for wrapping up on a wintry day.
✉ **2 Brompton Road** ☎ **0171-581 2151** Ⓟ **Knightsbridge**

## Cosmetics

### Crabtree & Evelyn
A byword for traditional English sophistication from the elegant old-fashioned shopfront to beautifully wrapped soaps and scents. Perfect for presents. Several branches.
✉ **239 Regent Street** ☎ **0171-409 1603** Ⓟ **Oxford Circus**

### Floris

Elegant and very up-market, London's oldest perfumery was established in 1730 and is a tourist attraction in its own right.

✉ **89 Jermyn Street** ☎ **0171-930 2885** 🚇 **Green Park**

### Lush

With its dynamic new style of packaging and serving potions and lotions, this groundbreaking store resembles a delicatessen more than a cosmetics shop.

✉ **7–11 Central Market, The Piazza, Covent Garden** ☎ **0171-240 4570** 🕐 **Daily**

### Neal's Yard Remedies

Delicious-smelling, stylis, Covent Garden herbalist, selling essential oils and homeopathic remedies of all kinds.

✉ **15 Neal's Yard** ☎ **0171-379 7222** 🚇 **Covent Garden**

### Penhaligon's

Beautiful Victorian shopfront and fittings with colognes and powders, perfumes and accessories. Several branches.

✉ **41 Wellington Street** ☎ **0171-836 2150** 🚇 **Covent Garden**

## Department Stores

### Fortnum & Mason

Predating the supermarket, the Fortnum & Mason's Food Hall has been supplying the nobility with parcels and hampers since the days of Queen Victoria and is the main attraction at this classy grocery emporium.

✉ **Piccadilly** ☎ **0171-734 8040** 🚇 **Piccadilly Circus, Green Park**

### Harrods

London's ultimate shopping experience (➤ 44).

✉ **Knightsbridge** ☎ **0171-730 1234** 🚇 **Knightsbridge** ❓ **Dress code: no scruffy attire, shorts, vests or backpacks**

### Harvey Nichols

Worth looking at for its renowned window displays 'Harvey Nicks' is the favourite shop of London's rich young things but also has a surprisingly good menswear department and a mouth-watering food hall.

✉ **87–135 Brompton Road** ☎ **0171-235 5000** 🚇 **Knightsbridge**

### Liberty

Famously associated with the art nouveau and developing design oriented printed fabrics, the interior of London's most beautiful store comprises series of four-storey galleries around a central well, draped with oriental carpets.

✉ **210–220 Regent Street** ☎ **0171-734 1234** 🚇 **Oxford Circus**

### Marks & Spencer

This is the biggest branch of one of Britain's favourite stores with consistently high quality and value across its range.

✉ **458 Oxford Street** ☎ **0171-935 7954** 🚇 **Marble Arch**

### Selfridges

The magnificent art deco and Ionic pillar frontage promises more than the store actually delivers. Probably best for clothes, though there's also a good food hall and a huge perfume department.

✉ **400 Oxford Street** ☎ **0171-62 9 1234** 🚇 **Bond Street**

### By Royal Appointment

Many of London's top shops claim a Royal Warrant of Appointment. These can only be granted by the Queen, the Queen Mother, the Prince of Wales and the Duke of Edinburgh and signifies that one of these members of the royal family has patronised the shop for at least three years. The coat (or coats) of arms on display outside the shop indicates which member.

# Furnishings, Food, Markets & Music

## Shop 'til you Drop
Serious shoppers should invest in the *Time Out Guide to Shopping & Services*. Equally useful to locals and visitors, it includes well over 1,000 reviews of all that's best in the capital and also features a 10 per cent discount card which may return your investment with interest.

## Design and Furnishings

### Conran Shop
Let style guru Sir Terence Conran council you on household accessories, furniture and food. Worth a visit for the splendid art deco building (▶ 92).
✉ **81 Fulham Road** ☎ **0171-589 7401** ⏰ **Daily (Sun noon–5:30)** 🚇 **South Kensington**

### Heal's
A wide range of furnishings and accessories that live up to the store's claim of 'style, quality and exclusivity' – but at a price.
✉ **196 Tottenham Court Road** ☎ **0171-636 1666** 🚇 **Goodge Street**

### Oxo Tower
Some of London's funkiest new designers show off their wares in equally stylish surroundings (▶ 63). Usually expensive, but good just to look at.
✉ **Oxo Tower Wharf, Riverside Walk/Bargehouse Street** ☎ **0171-401 3610** ⏰ **Tue–Sun 11–6** 🚇 **Waterloo**

## Food and Drink

### Berry Brothers & Rudd
One of London's most venerable and attractive shops, dating from the early 19th century, provides the perfect home for the quintessential traditional London wine merchant.
✉ **3 St James's Street** ☎ **0171-396 9600** 🚇 **Green Park**

### Fortnum & Mason (▶ 107)

### Neal's Yard Dairy
Splendid small rustic-style shop selling only British and Irish cheeses in tip-top condition.
✉ **17 Short's Gardens** ☎ **0171-379 7646** 🚇 **Covent Garden**

### Pâtisserie Valerie
This French pâtisserie in the heart of Soho is a London institution.
✉ **44 Old Compton Street** ☎ **0171-437 3466** ⏰ **Daily** 🚇 **Tottenham Court Road**

## Markets

### Berwick Street Market
The West End's best fruit and vegetable market is a boon to locals and self-catering visitors. Loud and lively stallholders and lots of local colour.
✉ **Berwick Street, Rupert Street** ⏰ **Mon–Sat 9–6** 🚇 **Leicester Square, Piccadilly Circus**

### Brick Lane
Get the real flavour of the East End with fruit and vegetables, clothes, bric-à-brac, oddities and pure junk. A great place for people-watching.
✉ **Brick Lane and environs** ⏰ **Sun 6am–1pm** 🚇 **Aldgate East, Shoreditch**

### Camden Lock
This is the arts and craft arm of the famous Camden Market (▶ 109), open during the week. Jewellery and clothing Saturday and Sunday. Good ethnic fast food, too.
✉ **Camden Lock Place, off Chalk Farm Road** ⏰ **Sat–Sun 10–6. Indoor stalls Tue–Sun 10–6** 🚇 **Camden Town**

## Camden Market

London's most colourful street market, famous for its street fashions, jewellery and ceramics, keeps growing. The latest offerings are 20th-century collectables and an organic food market. Great atmosphere.

✉ **Camden High Street**
🕐 **Thu–Sun 9–5:30**
🚇 **Camden Town**

## Covent Garden

The Jubilee Market for leather, clothes and cheap CDs Tues–Fri and crafts at weekends. The central Apple Market for arts and crafts. Antiques at both, Mondays.

✉ **Jubilee Market, The Piazza/Southampton Street; Apple Market, The Piazza**
🕐 **Both daily, 9–5**
🚇 **Covent Garden**

## Greenwich

A whole host of enjoyable lively weekend markets congregate around the main market hall off Greenwich Church Street. Sunday is best, when you'll find ethnic jewellery, pottery, antiques, clothes, arts, crafts and much more.

✉ **Around Greenwich Church Street/High Road and College Approach**
🕐 **Sat–Sun 9–5 (crafts market Sun only)**
🚇 **Greenwich mainline**

## Leadenhall Market

A classic Victorian glass and iron hall is the splendid home of the City's 600-year-old street market. Beautiful displays of fresh fish, game and poultry, meats and cheese, flowers and fruit.

✉ **Whittington Avenue, off Gracechurch Street**
🕐 **Mon–Fri 7–4**
🚇 **Monument, Bank**

## Petticoat Lane

London's best-known street market attracts tourist tat but there's plenty of worthwhile stuff here too, particularly leather goods.

✉ **Middlesex Street and environs**
🕐 **Sun 9–2 (Wentworth Street also open Mon–Fri 10–2:30)**
🚇 **Liverpool Street**

## Portobello Road

Around 2,000 antiques traders set up stall here every Saturday but elsewhere along this bustling mile-long stretch you'll find food, clothing and designer streetwear. Come on Saturday for buskers and reggae vibes.

✉ **Portobello Road and environs**
🕐 **General market Mon–Wed 9–5, Thu 9–1, Fri–Sat 7–6. Antiques Sat 7–6**
🚇 **Notting Hill Gate**

# Music

## Tower Records

The biggest and best of London's music megastores. Not only popular, chart stuff, but also excellent specialist, classical, jazz, folk and import departments.

✉ **1 Piccadilly Circus (branches at Queensway and Kensington High Street )**
☎ **0171-439 2500**
🕐 **Daily until midnight**
🚇 **Piccadilly Circus**

# Shoes

## Dr Marten's

The place to get London's most famous footwear. The five floors also include a large clothing department so the choice is extensive.

✉ **1–4 King Street**
☎ **0171-497 1460**
🕐 **Daily**
🚇 **Covent Garden**

## Tax-free Shopping

If you hold a non-EU passport then it is worth enquiring about the tax-free shopping export scheme which will enable you to claim back VAT (Value Added Tax) when you leave the country. This is currently rated at 17 per cent and is payable on most goods (books, food and children's clothes are the principal exceptions). All department stores and many other participating outlets (look for the TAX-FREE sticker) will give you details. Most will require a minimum purchase.

# Children's Attractions

## Look it Up

*Kid's Out* is the name of the excellent what's-on-for-children magazine published bi-monthly by *Time Out*. They also offer a telephone information service ☎ 0171-222 8070 Monday to Friday 4–6PM during term time, 9AM–4PM during holidays.

## Central London

### All Creatures Great and Small

The dinosaurs at the Natural History Museum (➤ 21) and the inmates of London Zoo (➤ 55) are perennial favourites. The new London Aquarium (➤ 51) is another good bet.

### Brass Rubbings

While Mum or Dad are admiring the churches of Westminster Abbey (➤ 26) and St Martin-in-the-Fields (➤ 75) the kids can make their own historical creation by rubbing wax crayons on to a sheet of paper on ancient (and not so ancient) church brasses.

### Covent Garden

You can't go wrong here with children. The pedestrianised central area has free outdoor entertainment, lots of informal eating choices, the London Transport Museum and the Cabaret Mechanical Theatre (➤ 18).

### Hands-on!

Many of London's major museums now have specific interactive exhibits for children. The best are at the Science Museum (➤ 23), London Transport Museum (➤ 54) and the National Maritime Museum (➤ 82).

### History in the Making

Family favourites include the Beefeaters with their blood 'n' thunder stories of the Tower of London (➤ 24); the historical spectacle and child-friendly actors of Hampton Court Palace (➤ 85) and the spectacular

hardware at the Imperial War Museum (➤ 46).

## Museums

### Bethnal Green Museum of Childhood

London's most comprehensive collection of toys, from all over the world, is well worth the detour.

✉ Cambridge Heath Road E2
🕐 Mon–Thu and Sat 10–5:50, Sun 2:30–5:50. Closed Fri
☎ 0181-983 5200, recorded information 0181-980 2415
🚇 Bethnal Green 🖐 Free

### London Toy and Model Museum

A superb collection of trains, teddies, dolls and thousands of other toys, all cleverly and inventively displayed.

✉ 21–23 Craven Hill, Paddington 🕐 Daily 9–5:30 (last admission 4:30) ☎ 0171-706 8000 🚇 Lancaster Gate, Paddington, Bayswater, Queensway 🖐 Moderate

### Pollock's Toy Museum

One of London's most charming (and most cramped) museums in London is crammed full of fascinating historic toys, games, childhood memora-bilia and miniature theatres.

✉ 1 Scala Street
🕐 Mon–Sat 10–5. Closed Sun, bank hols ☎ 0171-636 3452
🚇 Goodge Street 🖐 Cheap

### Ship Ahoy!

Clambering aboard deck is always a popular option and the older the vessel, the more the enjoyment. London has a number of historical ships including the *Cutty Sark* (➤ 84), *HMS Belfast* (➤ 44) and the *Golden Hinde*, a replica of Sir Francis

Drake's flagship. Any boat trip on the river – cruises depart from Westminster Pier (by Westminster Bridge) is also likely to be a child-pleaser.

✉ **Golden Hinde, St Mary Overie dock, beside Southwark Cathedral** 🕐 **May–Aug daily 10–4. Sep–Apr call for details** ☎ **0541-505041** 🚇 **London Bridge**

## Thrills...

### The Trocadero
Teenagers beat a path to the techno-thrills, white-knuckle, state-of-the-art motion-simulator rides and virtual reality adventures here. Expect long queues.

✉ **Piccadilly Circus** ☎ **0171-439 1791** 🕐 **Daily, 10AM–midnight/1AM daily** 🚇 **Piccadilly Circus**

## ... and Chills
The blood and gore of Madame Tussaud's Chamber of Horrors (➤ 56) and particularly the London Dungeon (➤ 54) are perennially popular with teenagers – but don't take young children.

## Restaurants
Older children and teenagers love Planet Hollywood and Thunder Drive at the Trocadero Centre while the Hard Rock Café (➤ 95) is an evergreen. Close by, on Shaftesbury Avenue, the Rainforest Café is a more ecologically friendly, jungle-themed restaurant for younger children.

### Smollensky's on the Strand
Come for lunch at the weekend when the special children's entertainment includes clowns, magic shows, face painting and Nintendo games.

✉ **105 Strand** ☎ **0171-497 2101** 🚇 **Embankment, Charing Cross**

## Shopping

### Hamley's
The world's greatest toy shop can be horribly busy (go on a weekday in term time if possible) but the range is enormous.

✉ **188–196 Regent Street** ☎ **0171-734 3161** 🚇 **Oxford Circus**

## Theatres

### Little Angel Theatre
Puppet shows every Saturday and Sunday at 11AM (for 3–6-year-olds) and 3PM (for older children). Additional shows during school holidays.

✉ **14 Dagmar Passage, off Cross Street, Islington** ☎ **0171-226 1787** 🚇 **Angel, Highbury & Islington**

### Unicorn Arts Theatre
Covers a wide range of activities including mime, puppets show and plays. Performances are at 11:30 and 2:30 on Sat and Sun with additional shows during holidays.

✉ **6–7 Great Newport Street** ☎ **0171-836 3334** 🚇 **Leicester Square**

## Outside London

### Windsor
Most kids will enjoy Windsor Castle (➤ 90), particularly its marvellous Dolls' House, but if the weather's good don't miss Legoland. This gloriously landscaped theme-park in miniature, designed for the under-12s, is one of the best children's attractions in the country. You'll need a full day to see it all.

✉ **Winkfield Road** 🕐 **Daily, Mid-Mar–Oct 10–6 (until 8 during school hols)** ☎ **0990-04 04 04** 💷 **Very expensive** 🚌 **Shuttle from Windsor town centre by castle.**

# Theatre

## What's On?

The listings on these pages contain only the best and the most famous of London's many entertainment options – which is a tiny proportion of the total offering. For the most comprehensive listing and best reviews buy *Time Out* magazine (aimed more at Londoners) or alternatively *What's On in London* (aimed more at visitors), both available weekly from most newsagents.

## The West End

Many West End theatres feature famous long-running musicals (*Miss Saigon*, *Cats*, *Les Misérables*, *Phantom of the Opera* and so on). Tickets for these are quite expensive and are usually scarce. If you have no luck at the box office, agents such as Ticketmaster (☎ 0171-344 444) or First Call (☎ 0171-497 9977) may be able to help – at a price. Never use touts.

A ticket booth on Leicester Square sells half-price tickets for that day's performance, though these are generally top-of-the range prices and not for the blockbuster shows.

### Society of London Theatres (SOLT) half-price ticket booth

✉ Leicester Square
🕐 Mon–Sat 12–6:30, Sun 12–3:30 for matinées only
💲 Cash (or theatre tokens) only. Service charge per ticket.
🚇 Leicester Square, Piccadilly Circus

### Shakespeare's Globe

See the plays of Shakespeare and his contemporaries as they were meant to be seen – outdoors, with no amplification, in daylight (or 'artificial daylight') and in all weathers. In the standing area of the Yard food and drink may be consumed during the performances and the audience is free to banter (within reason) with the players, as they did in the original Globe. This is great fun but beware, the Yard is uncovered and no umbrellas are allowed. (► 69).

✉ New Globe Walk, Bankside
☎ 0171-401 9919 or 0171-344 4444 (Ticketmaster, but no booking fee) 🕐 Season late May–late Sep 🚇 Mansion House, Cannon Street, London Bridge

### The Royal Shakespeare Company/The Barbican

The London home of the RSC is the Barbican Theatre, acclaimed for the design of its main theatre though not easy to find among the maze-like concrete ghetto that comprises the larger Barbican complex. A smaller theatre, the Pit, is also used for the plays of the Bard and others.

✉ Silk Street
☎ 0171-638 8891; recorded information 0171-328 7272
🚇 Barbican, Moorgate

### (Royal) National Theatre

The 'National' are resident at the South Bank Centre and are much admired for the outstanding quality of the serious work they produce in one of three theatres; the Olivier, the Lyttelton or the Cottesloe. All have productions in repertory.

✉ South Bank ☎ Box office 0171-928 2252; information 0171-633 0880 🚇 Waterloo
💲 A few discounted tickets for 'sell-out' productions are on sale on the day of performance. Get there early

### Regent's Park Open-air Theatre

This beautiful space has long been London's favourite al-fresco venue, staging plays (mostly by Shakespeare) and musicals.

✉ Inner Circle, Regent's Park
☎ 0171-486 2431/1933
🚇 Baker Street

# Dance & Music

## Dance

### Sadler's Wells Theatre
Rebuilt and reopened in late 1997, the theatre is the home of British contemporary dance. It also hosts touring international companies.
✉ **Rosebery Avenue** ☎ **0171-314 8800** 🚇 **Angel**

### South Bank Centre
The English National Ballet perform *The Nutcracker* in the Royal Festival Hall to full houses each January and return for a summer season. The South Bank also hosts top-class contemporary European dance groups.
✉ **South Bank** ☎ **0171-960 4242** 🚇 **Waterloo**

### Royal Ballet
The Royal Ballet are touring provincial venues until December 1999, while their home, the Royal Opera House, is rebuilt. See *Time Out* for details.

### The Coliseum
The English National Ballet perform at this beautiful venue during part of the summer (so too do the English National Opera).
✉ **St Martin's Lane** ☎ **0171-632 8300** 🚇 **Charing Cross, Leicester Square**

## Classical Music

### Barbican
The London Symphony Orchestra (LSO) and the English Chamber Orchestra are both resident at the Barbican, while the South Bank is a prime venue for orchestral and chamber music and recitals.
✉ **South Bank Centre** ☎ **Queen Elizabeth Hall/Royal**

Festival Hall 0171-960 4242, Purcell Room 0171-638 4141
🚇 **Waterloo**

### St John's
This deconsecrated baroque church is a superb setting for concerts, mostly of chamber music. Its Monday concert is broadcast live every week on BBC Radio 3.
✉ **Smith Square** ☎ **0171-222 1061** 🚇 **Westminster**

### Wigmore Hall
London's favourite small venue, recently refurbished, boasts near-perfect acoustics and attracts very high-quality chamber music and recitals. Its mid-morning Sunday concerts are particularly popular.
✉ **36 Wigmore Street** ☎ **0171-935 2141** 🚇 **Bond Street**

## Opera
While the Royal Opera House is being rebuilt (scheduled for completion December 1999) the Royal Opera company are touring various other London and provincial theatres. See *Time Out* for details. The English National Opera – who perform only in English – are resident at the London Coliseum.

## Jazz

### Jazz Café
This highly popular slick modern venue is home to many international jazz performers in the capital and also plays the contemporary sounds of Latin, funk, soul, hip-hop and blues.
✉ **5 Parkway, Camden Town** ☎ **0171-916 6060** 🚇 **Camden Town**

### Church Concerts
One of the most enjoyable ways to spend your lunchtime in London is to join the capital's office workers at a church concert. These are prevalent in the City of London but of particular note are the concerts at St Martin-in-the-Fields (▶ 75) and St James, Piccadilly (▶ 67). Lunchtime concerts are nearly always free, but do try to give a donation.

## Music Festivals

London boasts a lively calendar of musical events. On the classical side the most famous is the Proms (► 116), but others worth attending include the Covent Garden Festival (late May to early June), the Greenwich Festival (June) and the City of London Festival (June to July), which also includes jazz performers. See also Kenwood House (► 50).

The London International Jazz Festival lasts ten days in mid-November and the Capital Radio Music Festival (pop, rock, jazz, folk) is held in June and July.

### Jazz 'n' Pizza

London boasts two very high-quality jazz and pizza restaurants; the intimate Pizza Express and the spacious, more up-market Pizza on the Park.

✉ **Pizza Express, 10 Dean Street** ☎ **0171-439 8722** Ⓜ **Tottenham Court Road**
✉ **Pizza on the Park, 11 Knightsbridge** ☎ **0171-235 5273** Ⓜ **Hyde Park Corner**

### Ronnie Scott's

Small and smoky, this is *the* place to see the best jazz in the capital. There are generally two sets per night, at 10PM and after midnight.

✉ **47 Frith Street** ☎ **0171-439 0747. Book a table to be sure of a seat** Ⓜ **Leicester Square**

## Rock and Other Contemporary Music

Always at the cutting edge of many styles of pop and rock, London is a great place to see live music, from pokey, smoky pubs to the mega-venues such as Earl's Court and Wembley Stadium. Three of the best medium-sized places to see a band you've heard of are the Astoria, the Brixton Academy and the Forum (formerly the Town & Country Club). Get a copy of *Time Out* to see who's in town. A good time is usually guaranteed at the following venues

### Borderline

Lively basement with an eclectic musical booking policy, where you can catch up on a whole host of new sounds.

✉ **Orange Yard, off Manette Street** ☎ **0171-734 2095** Ⓜ **Tottenham Court Road**

### Dover Street

London's biggest live music restaurant, seating some 400 people, where the musical menu is jazz, blues, soul and R'n'B.

✉ **8–10 Dover Street** ☎ **0171-629 9813** Ⓜ **Green Park, Piccadilly Circus**

### Dublin Castle

Typically Camden, this dark and noisy pub is one of the best places in London to see lesser-known bands from a diverse range of backgrounds and styles.

✉ **94 Parkway** ☎ **0171-485 1773** Ⓜ **Camden Town**

### Half Moon, Putney

This is a famed music pub, just outside the centre but a great place to see up-and-coming rock and blues bands.

✉ **93 Lower Richmond Road SW15** ☎ **0181-780 9383** Ⓜ **Putney Bridge**

### Mean Fiddler

A little off the beaten track by central London standards but this northwest London venue is well worth the effort of seeking out to see first-class rock, folk, soul, roots and an eclectic range of world music.

✉ **24–28a Harlesden High Street NW10** ☎ **0181-963 0940** Ⓜ **Willesden Junction**

### Roadhouse

Heaving 1950s US-themed live-music bar with a thirtysomething crowd getting down to blues and rock'n'roll bands.

✉ **Jubilee Hall, 35, The Piazza, Covent Garden** ☎ **0171-240 6001** Ⓜ **Covent Garden**

# Nightclubs, Cinema & Sport

## Nightclubs

The London club scene is legendary, with many clubs changing themes throughout the week. See *Time Out* or *What's On in London* for details.

Tried and tested venues for older clubbers are Samantha's and Stringfellows. The most reliable of the new wave is the Ministry of Sound. Less intimidating to the casual clubber, though still very style conscious, are the Limelight, the Café de Paris, or Camden Palace. Other long-established venues are the Astoria and Gossips.

## Cinema

For mainstream blockbusters and premieres go to the Empire and the Odeon (avoid the adjacent cramped Odeon Mezzanine), both on Leicester Square; the ABC and the Curzon West End, both on Shaftesbury Avenue; or the Odeon Marble Arch with the city's biggest (conventional) screen. At the opposite end of the cinematic spectrum is the acclaimed National Film Theatre (NFT), at the South Bank. Look in *Time Out* for dozens of other interesting options around the capital.
✉ **National Film Theatre, South Bank** ☎ **0171-928 3232.** 🚇 **Waterloo**

### IMAX

For a truly spectacular wrap-around cinematic experience visit the Pepsi IMAX Cinema at the Trocadero, Piccadilly Circus (► 111) or the classier BFI London IMAX Cinema on the South Bank.

## Top Sporting Venues

### Football

#### Wembley Stadium
The spiritual home of English football. Hosts international matches, cup finals and many other events, including Rugby league finals and pop concerts.
✉ **Wembley Way** ☎ **0181-900 1234** 🚇 **Wembley Park, Wembley Central**

#### Arsenal Football Club
Very successful club, English Champions and FA Cup winners in 1998.
✉ **Highbury Stadium, Avenell Road 0171-413 3366** 🚇 **Arsenal**

#### Chelsea Football Club
European Cup Winner's Cup winners in 1998.
✉ **Stamford Bridge, Fulham Road** ☎ **0171-386 7799** 🚇 **Fulham Broadway**

#### Tottenham Hotspur Football Club
London's most glamorous under-achievers despite the big-name players.
✉ **White Hart Lane Stadium** ☎ **0181-365 5000** 🚇 **Seven Sisters,** 🚃 **White Hart Lane**

### Cricket

#### Lord's
Home of Middlesex County Cricket Club, the MCC and venue for test matches.
✉ **St John's Wood** ☎ **0171-289 1611** 🚇 **St John's Wood**

#### The Oval
Home of Surrey County Cricket Club and venue for test matches.
✉ **Kennington Oval** ☎ **0171-582 6660** 🚇 **Oval**

### Participatory Sports
At Hyde Park you can play tennis (near Lancaster Gate tube), go horse riding (☎ 0171-723 2813) or just jog. There are also tennis courts in Regent's Park. Swimmers should head for Marshall Street Leisure Centre, Soho; Porchester Spa at 225 Queensway, which includes Turkish baths; or the Oasis, Endell Street, Covent Garden. Should a heatwave hit town, it's worth noting that the latter has an outdoor pool, as does Hampstead Heath.

### Spectator Sports
In summer (June to late August) you can watch the quintessentially English game of cricket at Lord's or The Oval. In winter, football (soccer) is the national obsession, though for London's best (premier league) matches tickets are hard to get and very expensive. Another winter option is rugby union. See *Time Out* for details of all sporting events.

# What's On When

### Cockney Tradition
On the first Sunday in October, St Martin-in-the-Fields Church is packed for the Costermongers Harvest Festival Service. Costermongers were old London market traders who elected 'Pearly Kings and Queens' as representatives to safeguard their rights. These quintessential Cockney characters (a Cockney is a true indigenous Londoner) are a marvellous sight dressed in their traditional extravagant pearl-button suits.

### January/February
*Lord Mayor's Parade* (1 January) This procession of floats, bands and classic cars (from Westminster Bridge to Berkeley Square) attracts around a million onlookers. *Chinese New Year* (late January–early February). Human dragons and firecrackers light up Soho's Chinatown.

### March/April
*(University) Boat Race* (late March–early April): Oxford against Cambridge over 6km (4.2 miles) of the Thames from Putney to Mortlake. *Battersea Easter Show* (Easter Sunday and Monday): central London's best funfair with an Easter Parade on the Sunday afternoon. *London Marathon* (third week in April): some 30,000 runners, from world-class athletes to fancy-dressed 'fun-runners', pound the streets from Blackheath (Greenwich) to the Mall.

### May
*May Fayre and Puppet Festival* (Sunday nearest 9 May): an annual celebration of England's first recorded Punch and Judy Show, staged in Covent Garden in 1662. *Chelsea Flower Show* (late May): the world's best horticultural show, held in the grounds of the Royal Hospital.

### June/July
*Trooping the Colour* (second Saturday in June): an inspection and parade of the guards honours the Sovereign's official birthday (apply for tickets well in advance).

*Wimbledon Tennis Championship* (last week June, first week July): you can queue for early rounds but it's advance ticket-holders for the latter stages. *Henry Wood Promenade Concerts* (mid-July–mid-September): Britain's best-loved concert series occupies the Royal Albert Hall for three months.

### August
*Notting Hill Carnival* (August bank holiday weekend): Rio comes to London with the biggest street festival in Europe.

### September
*Festival of Street Theatre* (second and third week): a great time to be in Covent Garden. *Thames Festival:* a new celebration on the South Bank of the river, culminating with spectacular fireworks.

### October–December
*State Opening of Parliament* (late October–early November): pomp and ceremony as the Queen arrives at Parliament in the Gold Coach. *London-to-Brighton Veteran Car Run* (first Sunday in November): a great spectacle as Hyde Park is crammed with Chitty Chitty Bang Bang lookalikes. *Lord Mayor's Show* (second Saturday in November): London's best traditional street parade, from Mansion House to the Royal Courts of Justice. *Christmas Lights* (mid-November–early January): Regent Street and Oxford Street glow with the latest festive creations.

# Practical
# Matters

Above: *revellers in Trafalgar Square*
Right: *a Horse Guard*

# TIME DIFFERENCES

**GMT**
12 noon

**London**
12 noon

→
**Germany**
1PM

←
**USA (NY)**
7AM

→
**Netherlands**
1PM

→
**Spain**
1PM

# BEFORE YOU GO

## WHAT YOU NEED

- ● Required
- ○ Suggested
- ▲ Not required

|  | UK | Germany | USA | Netherlands | Spain |
|---|---|---|---|---|---|
| Passport/National Identity Card | ▲ | ● | ● | ● | ● |
| Visa | ▲ | ▲ | ▲ | ▲ | ▲ |
| Onward or Return Ticket | ▲ | ○ | ○ | ○ | ○ |
| Health Inoculations (tetanus and polio) | ▲ | ▲ | ▲ | ▲ | ▲ |
| Health Documentation (➤ 123, Health) | ▲ | ▲ | ● | ● | ● |
| Travel Insurance | ○ | ○ | ○ | ○ | ○ |
| Driving Licence (national) | ● | ● | ● | ● | ● |
| Car Insurance Certificate | ▲ | ● | ● | ● | ● |
| Car registration document | ▲ | ● | ● | ● | ● |

## WHEN TO GO

**London**

| ███████ | High season |
| ⬜ | Low season |

| 6°C | 7°C | 10°C | 13°C | 17°C | 20°C | 22°C | 22°C | 19°C | 14°C | 10°C | 7°C |
|---|---|---|---|---|---|---|---|---|---|---|---|
| JAN | FEB | MAR | APR | MAY | JUN | JUL | AUG | SEP | OCT | NOV | DEC |

 Very wet  Wet  Cloud  Sun  Sun/Showers

## TOURIST OFFICES

**In the USA**
Suite 701
551 Fifth Avenue
New York
NY 10176
☎ 212/986 2266

Suite 1510
625 N Michegan Ave
Chicago
IL 60611
(personal callers only)

**In Canada**
Suite 450
111 Avenue Road
Toronto
Ontario
M5R 3J8
☎ 416-961 8124
fax: 416-961 2175

118

POLICE 999

FIRE 999

AMBULANCE 999

## WHEN YOU ARE THERE

### ARRIVING

There are direct flights to London from all over the world. London has two main airports, Heathrow and Gatwick, with smaller airports at Luton, Stansted and London City (Docklands). There are train links to Paris and Brussels, and good road links to the Channel ports.

| London Heathrow Airport | Journey Times |
|---|---|
| Kilometres to city centre | 🚆 60 minutes |
|  | 🚌 40 minutes |
| **25 kilometres** | 🚗 40 minutes |

| London Gatwick Airport | Journey times |
|---|---|
| Kilometres to city centre | 🚆 30 minutes |
|  | 🚌 70–90 minutes |
| **48 kilometres** | 🚗 60–75 minutes |

### MONEY

Britain's currency is the pound (£), issued in notes of £5, £10, £20 and £50. There are 100 pennies or pence (p) to each pound and coins come in denominations of 1p, 2p, 5p, 10p, 20p, 50p, £1 and £2. Travellers' cheques may be accepted by some hotels, shops and restaurants. Travellers' cheques in pounds are the most convenient. Bureaux de change are common in central London, but they often offer poorer rates of exchange.

### TIME

 London is on Greenwich Mean Time (GMT) in winter, but from late March until late October British Summer Time (BST, ie GMT+1) operates.

### CUSTOMS

 **YES**

**Goods obtained Duty Free inside the EU or goods bought outside the EU (Limits):**
Alcohol (over 22% vol): 1L or Alcohol (not over 22% vol): 2L *and*
Still table wine: 2L,
Cigarettes: 200 *or* Cigars: 50 *or* Tobacco: 250gms
Perfume: 60ml
Toilet water: 250ml
**Goods bought Duty and Tax Paid for own use inside the EU (Guidance Levels):**
Alcohol (over 22% vol): 10L
Alcohol (not over 22% vol): 20L *and* Wine (max 60L sparkling): 90L Beer: 110L
Cigarettes: 800, Cigars: 200, Tobacco: 1kg
Perfume and Toilet Water: no limit
**You must be 17 or over to benefit from alcohol and tobacco allowances.**

 **NO**

Unlicensed drugs, firearms, ammunition, offensive weapons, obscene material, unlicensed animals, counterfeit and copied goods, meat and poultry.

119

## EMBASSIES AND CONSULATES

**Germany**
0171-824 1300

**USA**
0171-499 9000

**Netherlands**
0171-584 5040

**Spain**
0171-235 5555

## WHEN YOU ARE THERE

### TOURIST OFFICES

**London Tourist Board Tourist Offices** (personal callers only, no telephone or fax enquiries):

- Victoria Station Forecourt

- Heathrow Terminals 1, 2, 3 Underground Station

- Heathrow Terminal 3 Arrivals Concourse

- Liverpool Street Station

- Selfridge's, Oxford Street

- Waterloo International Station, Arrivals Hall

- British Travel Centre, 12 Regent Street

- Hay's Galleria, Tooley Street, Southwark

**Other offices**
- City of London
St Paul's Churchyard
☎ 0171-332 1456

- Richmond
Old Town Hall, Whittaker Avenue
☎ 0181-940 9125

- Twickenham
The Atrium, Civic Centre, York Street
☎ 0181-891 7272

### NATIONAL HOLIDAYS

| J | F | M | A | M | J | J | A | S | O | N | D |
|---|---|---|---|---|---|---|---|---|---|---|---|
| 2 | (1) | 1(3) | (1) | 1 | 1 | | 1 | | 1 | | 2 |

| | |
|---|---|
| 1 Jan | New Year's Day |
| Mar/Apr | Good Friday, Easter Monday |
| First Mon May | May Day Bank Holiday |
| Last Mon May | Late May Bank Holiday |
| Last Mon in August | August Bank Holiday |
| 25 Dec | Christmas Day |
| 26 Dec | Boxing Day |

Almost all attractions close on Christmas Day. On other holidays some attractions open, often with reduced hours. There are no general rules regarding the opening times of restaurants and shops, so check before making a special journey.

### OPENING HOURS

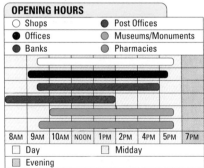

The times shown above are traditional opening hours. Many shops in the West End open for longer hours and also on Sunday. High Street banks are open Saturday morning and bureaux de change are open daily until late. Smaller museums may close one day a week. When pharmacies are closed a sign in the window gives details of the nearest one that is on 24-hour duty.

**DRIVE ON THE
LEFT**

**TOILETS
CHARGE**

## PUBLIC TRANSPORT

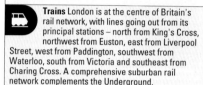

Internal flights link Northern Ireland, Scotland, Wales and the regions with many of London's airports. London City Airport is in Docklands, less than 10km (6 miles) from the City financial district.

**Trains** London is at the centre of Britain's rail network, with lines going out from its principal stations – north from King's Cross, northwest from Euston, east from Liverpool Street, west from Paddington, southwest from Waterloo, south from Victoria and southeast from Charing Cross. A comprehensive suburban rail network complements the Underground.

**Buses** London's famous red double-decker buses cover the capital in a dense network of services. A red bus stop symbol on a white background indicates that the bus must stop here (unless it is full); at a white symbol on a red background you must hail the bus by putting out an arm. Pay on board.

River transport on the Thames is not as well used as it might be and regular services have a chequered history, but sightseeing boats are frequent, popular and offer some of London's most memorable views.

**Underground** The underground, or tube, is by far the quickest way to get around London. Underground maps (► 72) are on display at stations, on platforms and on the trains themselves, and lines are named and colour-coded for ease of reference. Tube trains run from around 5:30AM to midnight or later.

## CAR RENTAL

The leading international car rental companies have offices at all London airports and you can book a car in advance. Local companies offer competitive rates and will deliver a car to the airport .

## TAXIS

London's famous licensed black cabs (which confusingly also come in various other colours) are very reliable with specially trained drivers. Hail them in the street when the yellow 'For Hire' sign on the roof is lit.

## DRIVING

Speed limit on motorways and dual carriageways: **70mph (112kph)**

Speed limit on main roads: **50–60mph (80–100kph)**

Speed limit on minor roads: **30–40mph (50–65kph)**

Must be worn in front seats at all times and in rear seats where fitted.

Random breath tests are carried out frequently, especially late at night. The limit is 35 micrograms of alcohol in 100ml of breath.

Fuel is sold in litres and available as unleaded or 4-star petrol or diesel. 4-star will not be available after Jan 2000. In central London, petrol stations are few and far between but there are many open 24 hours on the main roads leading away from the centre and in the suburbs.

If you break down driving your own car and are a member of an AA-affiliated motoring club, you can call the AA (☎ 0800 887 766 free phone). If your car is hired, follow the instructions given in the documentation; most rental firms provide a rescue service.

At the top of the page is a ruler showing CENTIMETRES (0–8) and INCHES (0–3).

## PERSONAL SAFETY

London is generally a safe city and policemen are often seen on the beat (walking the streets) in the central areas. They are usually friendly and very approachable.

To help prevent crime:

- Do not carry more cash than you need
- Beware of pickpockets in markets, on the underground, in tourist sights or crowded places
- Avoid walking alone in dark alleys at night

**Police assistance:**
☎ **999**
**from any call box**

## TELEPHONES

which phone company is operating them. Coin-operated telephones take 10p, 20p, 50p and £1 coins, but card-operated phones are often more convenient. Phonecards are available from many shops. Hotel phones are very expensive. To call the operator dial 100.

The traditional red phone boxes are now rare; instead, kiosks come in a wide variety of different designs and colours, depending on

| International Dialling Codes | |
| --- | --- |
| **From London to:** | |
| **Germany:** | 00 49 |
| **USA:** | 00 1 |
| **Canada:** | 00 1 |
| **Netherlands:** | 00 31 |
| **Spain:** | 00 34 |

## POST

Post offices are open Mon–Fri 9–5.30, Sat 9–1. The only exception is Trafalgar Square Post Office, 24–28 William IV Street, open Mon–Thu and Sat 8–8, Fri 8.30–8. Post restante mail may also be sent here.

## ELECTRICITY

The power supply in Britain is 240 volts.

Sockets only accept three (square)-pin plugs, so an adaptor is needed for Continental and US appliances. A transformer is needed for appliances operating on 110-120 volts.

## TIPS/GRATUITIES

| Yes ✓ No ✗ | | |
| --- | --- | --- |
| Restaurants (service not included) | ✓ | 10% |
| Tour Guides | ✓ | £1–2 |
| Hairdressers | ✓ | 10% |
| Taxis | ✓ | 10% |
| Chambermaids | ✓ | 50p–£1 per day |
| Porters | ✓ | 50p–£1 depending on number of bags |

**Light**: London is not renowned for its bright sunshine and the tall buildings create a lot of shadow, so pack plenty of 200 ASA-speed film.
**Where you can photograph**: Most museums will not allow you to take pictures. Check first.
**Where to buy film**: Film and camera batteries are readily available from tourist shops. Rapid-developing services are also widely available.

## HEALTH

### Insurance
Nationals of EU and certain other countries can get medical treatment in Britain with the relevant documentation, although private medical insurance is still advised, and is essential for all other visitors.

### Dental Services
Emergency dental treatment may be available free of charge if you can find a National Health dentist willing to treat you. A list can be found in the yellow pages. Dental treatment should be covered by private medical insurance.

### Weather
Although not renowned for its sunny weather, the sun can shine a lot in July and August, when many Londoners take to the parks to sunbathe. Some sights involve being outdoors for prolonged periods when you should 'cover up', apply sunscreen and drink plenty of water.

### Drugs
Prescription and non-prescription drugs and medicines are available from chemists/pharmacies. Pharmacists can advise on medication for common ailments. Chemists operate a rota so there will always be one that is open 24 hours; notices in all pharmacy windows give details.

### Safe Water
Tap water is safe to drink. Mineral water is widely available but is often expensive, particularly in restaurants.

## CONCESSIONS

**Students and Senior Citizens** Senior Citizens and holders of an International Student Identity Card will be able to obtain some concessions on travel and entrance fees. There are a handful of good youth hostels in London (➤ 102).

**The White Card** The London White Card is a pass to 15 of the capital's top museums and galleries, including the V&A, the Science Museum, the Natural History Museum, and the Museum of the Moving Image. It is valid for three or seven days and can be bought in some shops and tourist information centres.

## CLOTHING SIZES

| UK | Rest of Europe | USA | | |
|---|---|---|---|---|
| 36 | 46 | 36 | | Suits |
| 38 | 48 | 38 | | |
| 40 | 50 | 40 | | |
| 42 | 52 | 42 | | |
| 44 | 54 | 44 | | |
| 46 | 56 | 46 | | |
| 7 | 41 | 8 | | Shoes |
| 7.5 | 42 | 8.5 | | |
| 8.5 | 43 | 9.5 | | |
| 9.5 | 44 | 10.5 | | |
| 10.5 | 45 | 11.5 | | |
| 11 | 46 | 12 | | |
| 14.5 | 37 | 14.5 | | Shirts |
| 15 | 38 | 15 | | |
| 15.5 | 39/40 | 15.5 | | |
| 16 | 41 | 16 | | |
| 16.5 | 42 | 16.5 | | |
| 17 | 43 | 17 | | |
| 8 | 34 | 6 | | Dresses |
| 10 | 36 | 8 | | |
| 12 | 38 | 10 | | |
| 14 | 40 | 12 | | |
| 16 | 42 | 14 | | |
| 18 | 44 | 16 | | |
| 4.5 | 38 | 6 | | Shoes |
| 5 | 38 | 6.5 | | |
| 5.5 | 39 | 7 | | |
| 6 | 39 | 7.5 | | |
| 6.5 | 40 | 8 | | |
| 7 | 41 | 8.5 | | |

# WHEN DEPARTING

- Remember to contact the airport on the day before leaving to ensure the flight details are unchanged.
- If travelling by ferry you must check-in no later than the time specified on your ticket.

## LANGUAGE

The language spoken by Londoners is as varied as the ethnic and cultural backgrounds from which they come. You will hear many varied accents in the centre especially amongst bar and restaurant staff.

Of the 'London English' there is a range from 'BBC-English' (the kind spoken with perfect clarity and precision favoured by the BBC) to the broad Cockney dialect of the East End. Made famous by the likes of Henry Higgins, or rather '*Enry 'Iggins* in *My Fair Lady*, Cockney cuts out the 'h' at the start of words, and the final 'g' from words which end -ing. Statements of fact are also often confirmed by the use of the term 'innit?' (isn't it?).

The most famous aspect of the Cockney language is rhyming slang, an insiders vocabulary which was developed among street traders for clandestine communication, for example telephone becomes 'dog and bone', and may be abbreviated just to 'dog'! Below are a few examples. You may hear the occasional word in a local's pub or shouted out at street markets. In the latter case it may well be tongue-in-cheek – a touch of local colour put on specially for British tourists as much as foreign visitors.

Don't worry if you don't get it. Most Londoners will be equally baffled! If you want to delve more deeply, however, you'll find whole books and even mini-dictionaries devoted to the language of Cockney rhyming slang.

### Common Cockney rhyming slang

| | |
|---|---|
| apples and pears | stairs |
| barnet (fair) | hair |
| boat(race) | face |
| daisy roots | boots |
| dog and bone | telephone |
| (h)'alf inch | pinch, steal |
| 'ampstead 'eef | teeth |
| have a butcher's (hook) | to have a look |
| jam jar | car |
| loaf (of bread) | head |
| mince pies | eyes |
| my old china (plate) | mate, friend |
| plates (of meat) | feet |
| porky (pie) | lie |
| rabbit (and pork) | talk, chatter– usually meaningless |
| rubadubdub | public house |
| tea leaf | thief |
| titfer (tat) | hat |
| touble (and strife)/Duchess (of Fife) | wife |
| two an' eight | state/mood |
| whistle (and flute) | suit |

### Other common colloquialisms to be heard in London

| | |
|---|---|
| Awright mate? | How are you? |
| boozer | pub (or person who drinks heavily) |
| bobby, copper, the (old) Bill | policeman |
| bovver | trouble, fighting |
| chippy | fish and chip shop |
| a face | a well-known person |
| geezer | man, person |
| guv | boss |
| fag | cigarette |
| innit | isn't it (at end of sentence and not meant as a question) |
| leave it out! | stop it |
| scarper | to run away |
| the smoke | London |
| the sticks | the provinces (anywhere outside London) |
| straight up | honest |
| sussed out | found out |
| wotcher mate | another familiar term of greeting |
| would you adam and eve it? | Would you believe it? |

**Acknowledgements**
The Automobile Assocation wishes to thank the following photographers, libraries and associations for their assistance in the preparation of this book:

BANK OF ENGLAND 32b; BANQUETING HOUSE 33; BRITISH MUSEUM, LONDON 17b; MARY EVANS PICTURE LIBRARY 10b, 11; MUSEUM OF LONDON 57b; NATIONAL ARMY MUSEUM 59b; PICTURES COLOUR LIBRARY F/Cover c; REX FEATURES 14c; THE RITZ, LONDON 60c; SPECTRUM COLOUR LIBRARY 24b, 43b; V&A MUSEUM, LONDON 25b;

The remaining photographs are held in the Association's own library (AA PHOTO LIBRARY) with contributions from the following photographers:
13c, 51c, 74, 91a, 92/116 (S Bates); 15b (T Cohen); 8c, 23b (R Day); 88b (S L Day); 13b, 39, 42a, 44, 47b, 49a, 49b, 54, 56b, 64c, 68a, 68b, 69a, 79, 80, 81, 84a, 88a, 89 (P Kenward); 2, 18b, 64b, 117a, 117b (J McMillan); 36b, 77b, 82 (S & O Mathews); 6b, 8b, 9c, 52c, 53b, 61b, 65b, 87, 122b (R Mort); 5a, 6a, 7a, 7b, 8a, 9a, 10a, 12a, 13a, 14a, 15a, 16a, 17a, 18a, 19a, 20a, 21a, 22a, 23a, 24a, 25a, 26a, 46 (B Smith); B/Cover, 1, 9b, 27b, 35b, 40, 45, 51b, 52b, 55, 65a, 75, 90, 122a, 122c (R Strange); 21b, 26b, 37b, 50b, 69b, 70, 86a (J A Tims); 5b, 67b, 85 (M Trelawny); F/Cover a, b, 22b, 30, 31a, 31b, 32a, 35a, 36a, 37a, 38a, 41a, 43a, 47a, 50a, 51a, 52a, 53a, 56a, 57a, 58a, 59a, 60a, 61a, 61c, 62a, 64a (R Victor); F/ Cover d, 6c, 19b, 20b, 34, 38b, 41b, 48, 58b, 63, 66, 77a, 83, 84b, 86b (W Voysey); 27a, 28, 29, 67a, 71, 91b (P Wilson); 42b, 76, 78 (T Woodcock); 12b, 16/17, 62b (G Wrona)

**Copy editor:** Rebecca Snelling   **Page layout:** Design 23